RECORDED VERSIONS GUITAR

AUTHENTIC TRANSCRIPTIONS WITH NOTES AND TABLATURE

Steve Vai the Ultra Zone

Music transcriptions by Pete Billmann, Colin Higgins and Jeff Jacobson

ISBN 0-634-01284-3

HAL•LEONARD®
CORPORATION

7777 W. BLUEMOUND RD. P.O. BOX 13819 MILWAUKEE, WI 53213

Visit Hal Leonard Online at
www.halleonard.com
www.vai.com

Photo by Richard Pike • Illustration by Aaron Brown

Photo by Richard Pike • Illustration by Aaron Brown

Photo by Richard Pike • Illustration by Aaron Brown

Guitar Notation Legend

BEND: Strike note and bend upwards. Numbers over TAB indicate the degree of pitch shift by a bend in terms of fret position.

BEND AND RELEASE: Strike and bend upwards, then release the bend back to the original note. only the first note is struck.

GRADUAL BEND: Bend up to the specified pitches while striking notes in the rhythm indicated.

PREBEND: Bend the note upwards, then strike it.

PREBEND AND RELEASE: Bend the note upwards, then strike it and release the bend to the original note.

VIBRATO: The string is vibrated by rapidly bending and releasing the note with the left hand or vibrato bar. w/ bar means "with bar"

WIDE OR EXAGGERATED VIBRATO: The pitch is varied to a greater degree by vibrating with the left hand or vibrato bar.

VIBRATO BAR: The pitch of the note or chord is dropped or raised using the vibrato bar

MUFFLED STRINGS: A percussive sound is made by laying the left hand across the strings without depressing them with the right hand

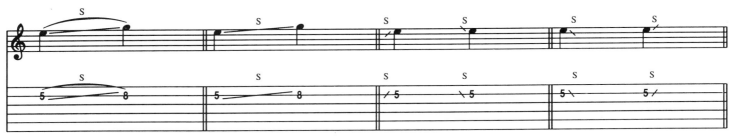

SLIDE: Strike the first note and then slide the the same hand up or down to the second note. The second note is not struck.

SLIDE: Same as before, except the second note is struck.

SLIDE: Slide up or down to the note indicated from a few frets below or above.

SLIDE: Strike the note and slide up or down an indefinite number of frets, releasing finger pressure at the end of the slide.

PALM MUTING: The note is muted by the lightly touching the string(s) just before the bridge.

HAMMER-ON: Without picking, sound the note indicated by sharply fretting the note with a left-hand finger.

HAMMER-ON: Strike the first (lower) note, then sound the higher note with another finger by fretting it without picking.

PULL-OFF: Place both fingers on the notes to be sounded. Strike the first note and without picking, pull the finger off to sound the second (lower) note.

RHYTHM SLASHES: Strum chords in the rhythm indicated. Use chord voicings found in the fingering diagrams at the top of the first page of each song.

PICK SLIDE: The edge of the pick is rubbed down or up the length of the string(s) producing a scratch sound.

TRILL: Very rapidly alternate between the 2 notes in parenthesis by hammering on and pulling off.

TAPPING: Hammer (tap) the fret indicated with the appropriate right-hand finger and pull off to the note indicated by the left hand.

The Blood & Tears

By Steve Vai

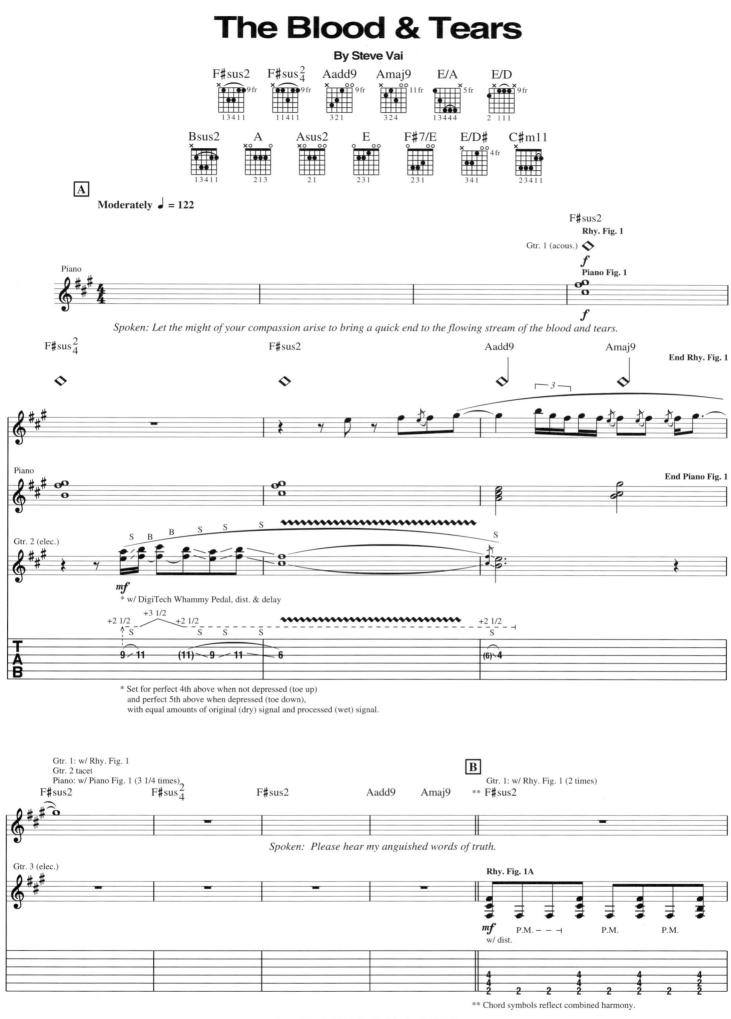

Spoken: An ocean of measureless qualities in an ocean of joy.

Spoken: We love compassion.

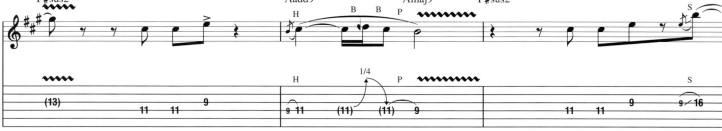

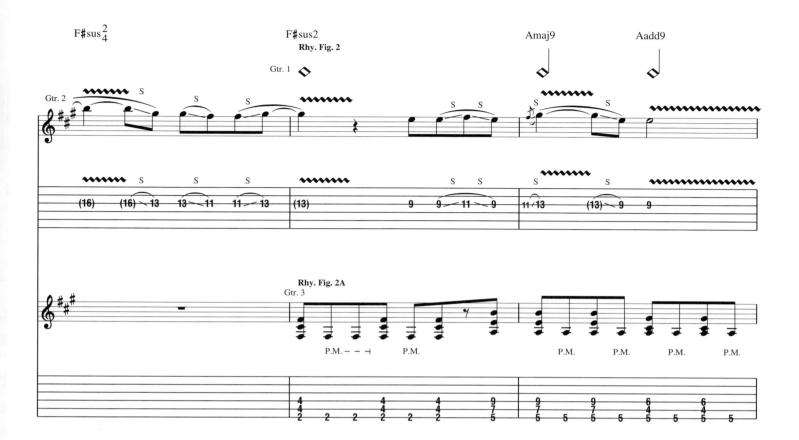

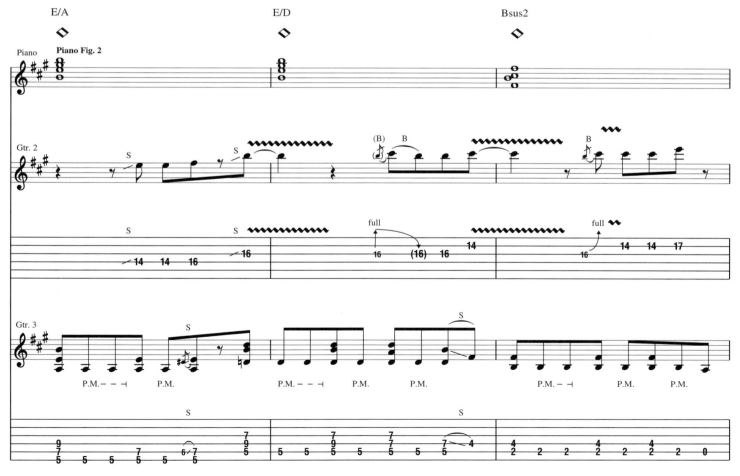

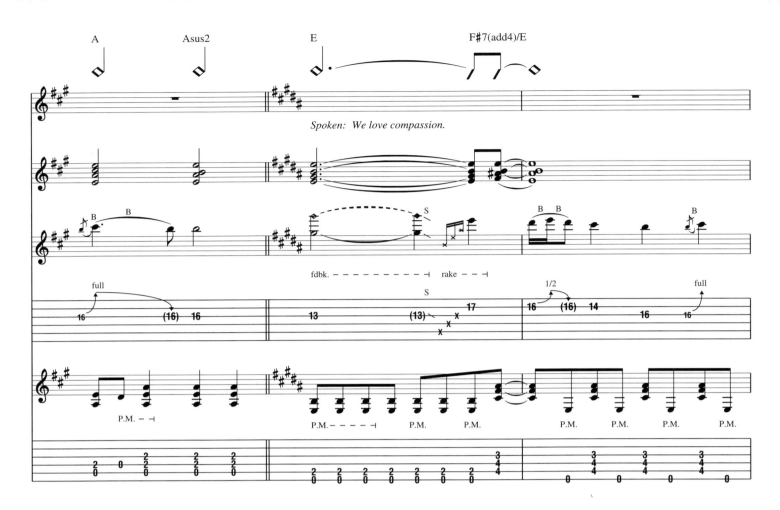

Spoken: We love compassion.

* Key signature denotes F# Mixolydian.

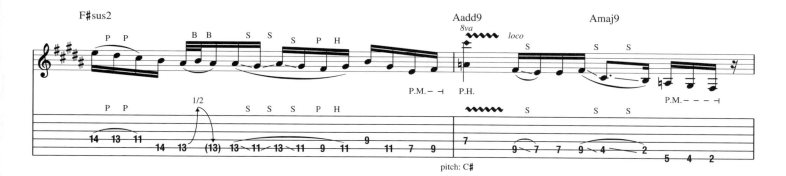

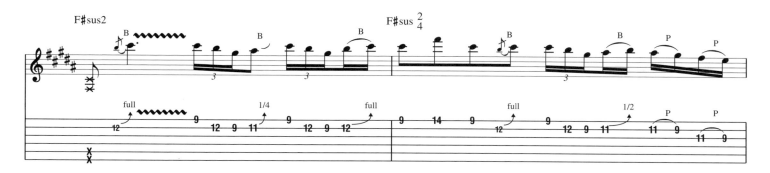

pitch: C#

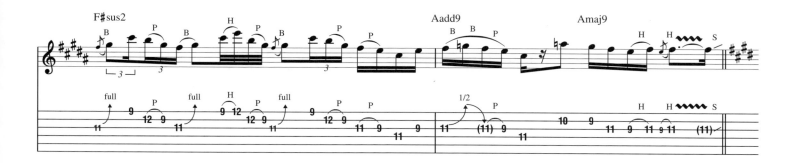

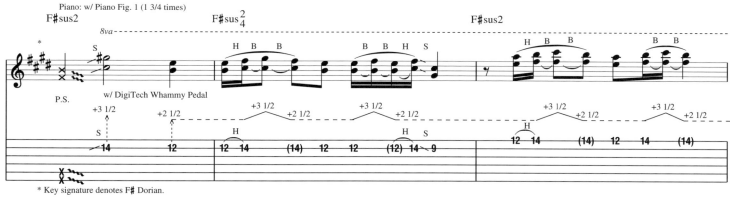

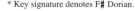

* Key signature denotes F# Dorian.

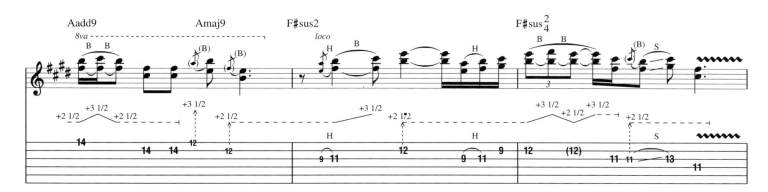

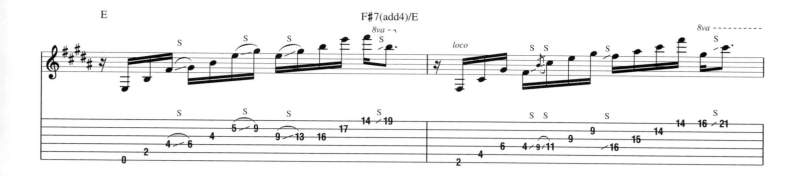

E   F#7(add4)/E

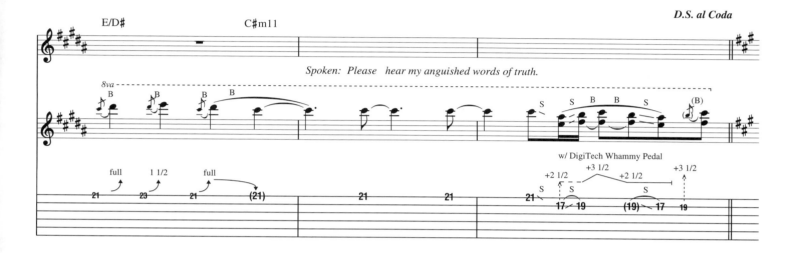

E/D#   C#m11

D.S. al Coda

Spoken: Please hear my anguished words of truth.

w/ DigiTech Whammy Pedal

⊕ **Coda**

F

Gtrs. 1 & 3 tacet

N.C.

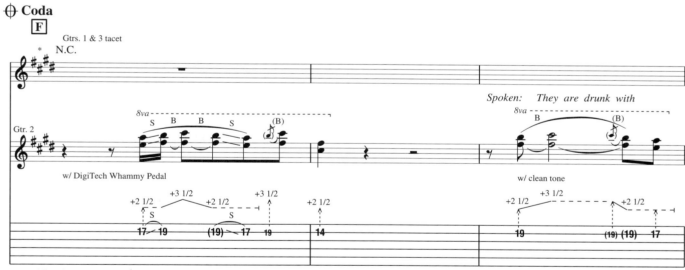

Gtr. 2

w/ DigiTech Whammy Pedal

Spoken: They are drunk with

w/ clean tone

*Key signature denotes F# Dorian.

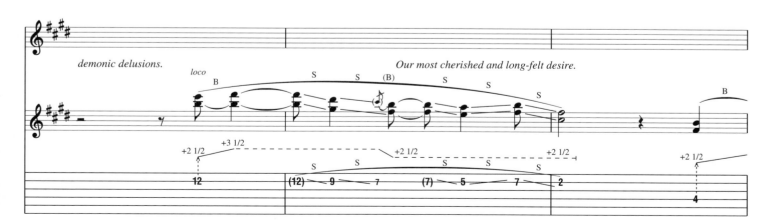

demonic delusions.

Our most cherished and long-felt desire.

Vocal: w/ Vocal Fig. 1 (2 times)
Gtrs. 1 & 3: w/ Rhy. Figs. 1 & 1A (6 3/4 times)
Piano: w/ Piano Fig. 1 (7 1/4 times)

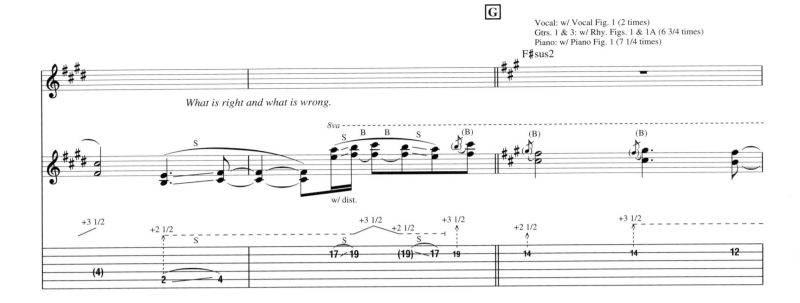

What is right and what is wrong.

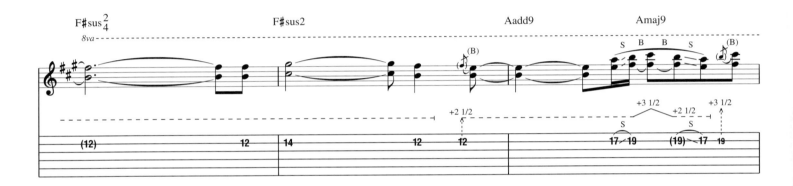

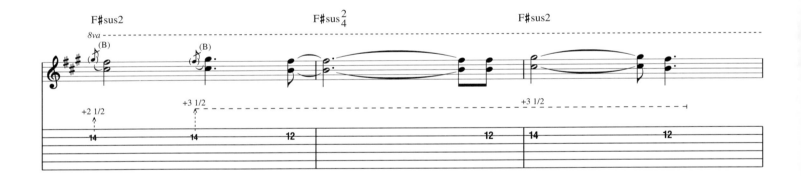

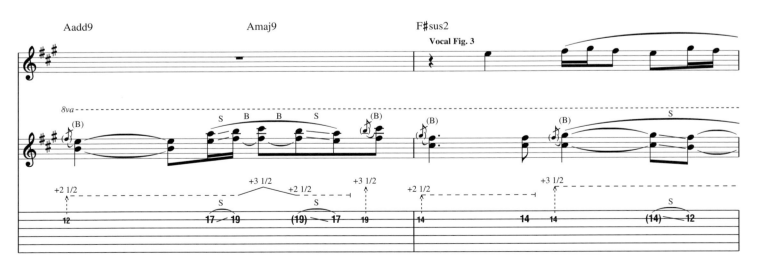

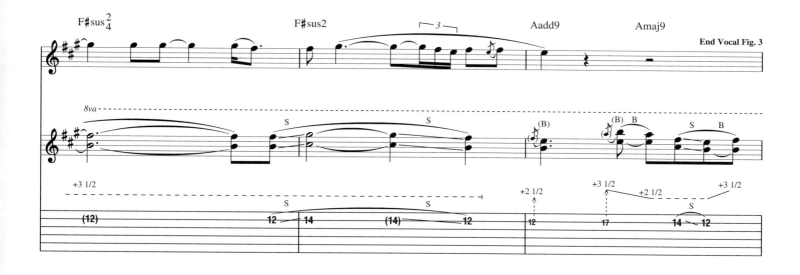

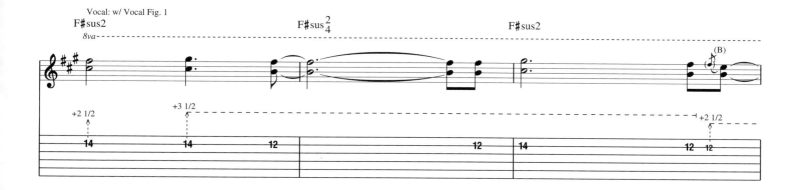

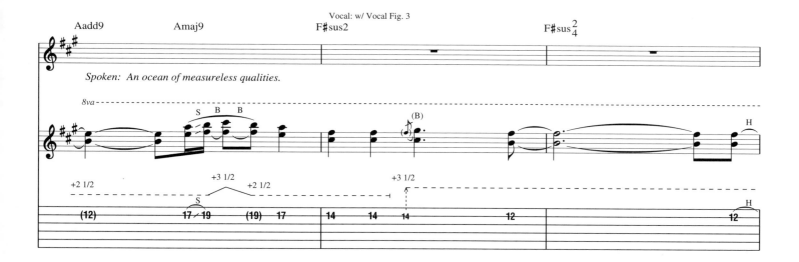

Spoken: An ocean of measureless qualities.

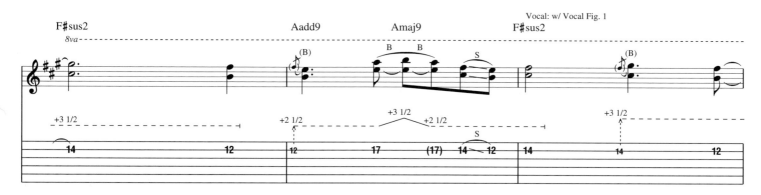

Spoken: In an ocean of joy.

Spoken: Please hear my anguished

words of truth.

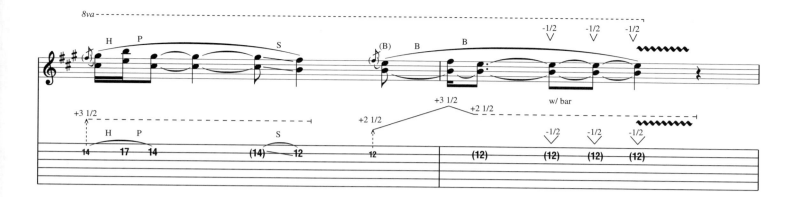

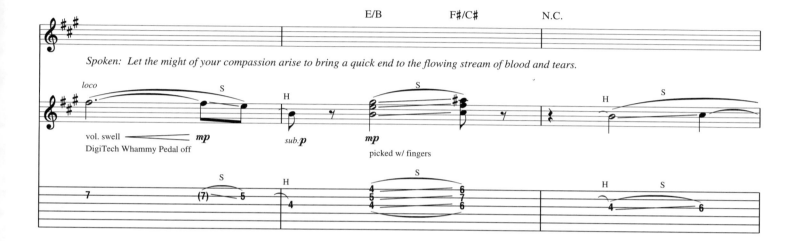

Spoken: *Let the might of your compassion arise to bring a quick end to the flowing stream of blood and tears.*

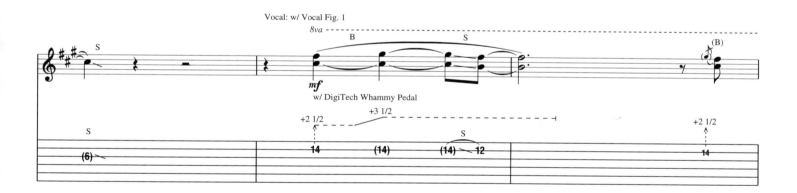

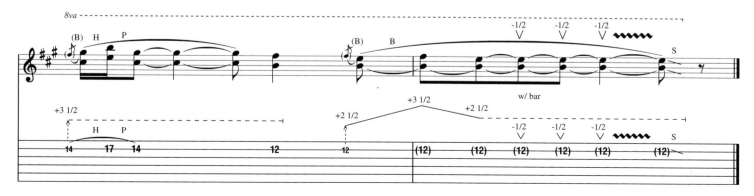

The Ultra Zone

By Steve Vai

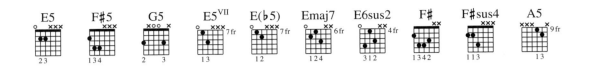

*Key signature denotes A Mixolydian.

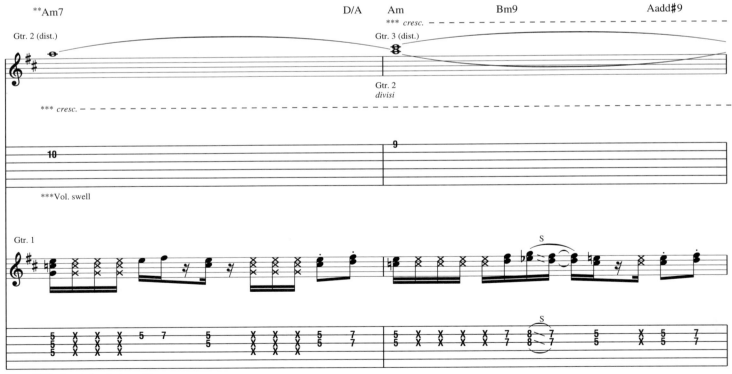

**Chord symbols reflect overall harmony.

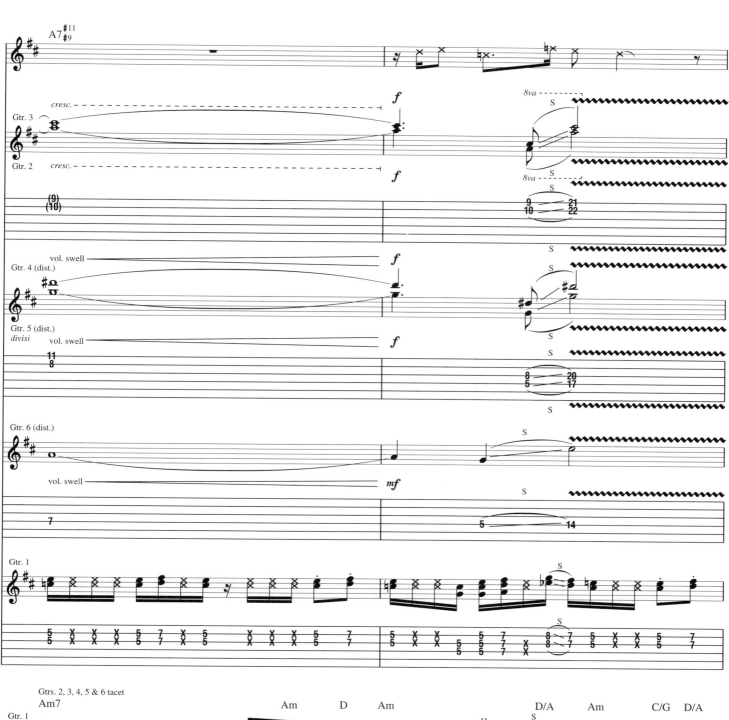

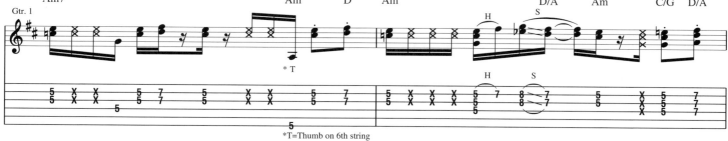

*T=Thumb on 6th string

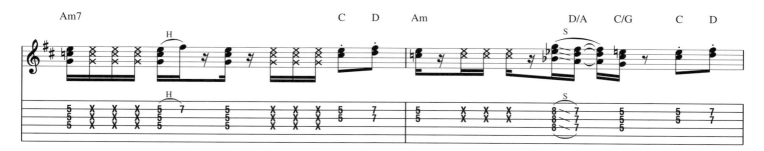

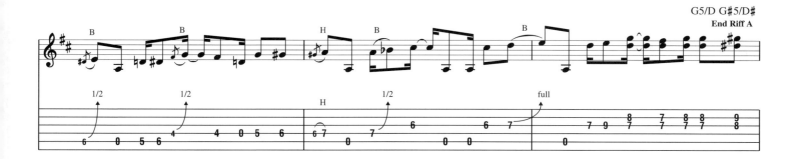

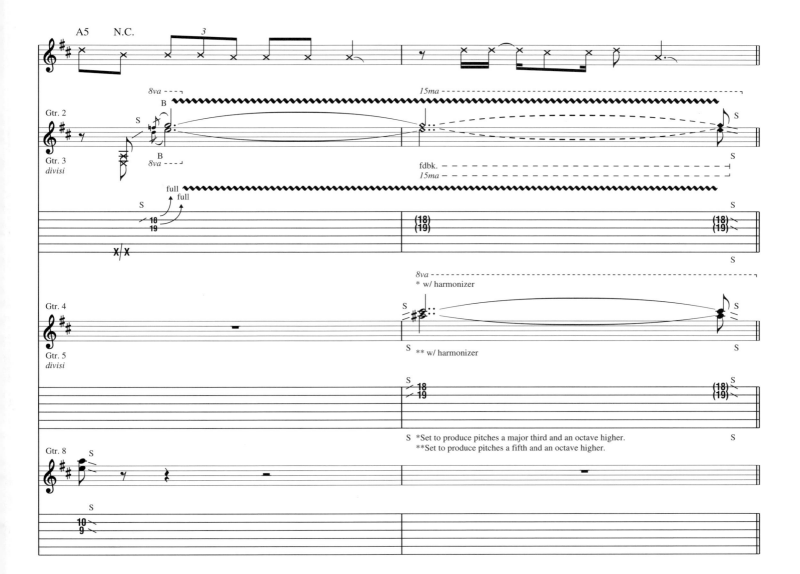

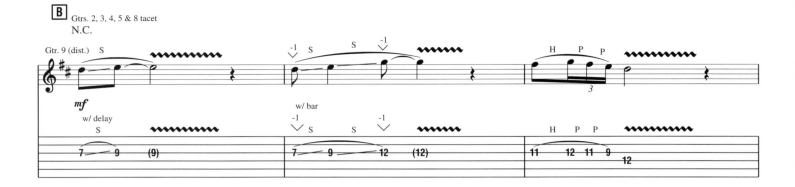

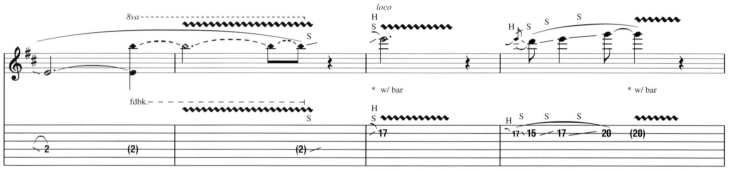

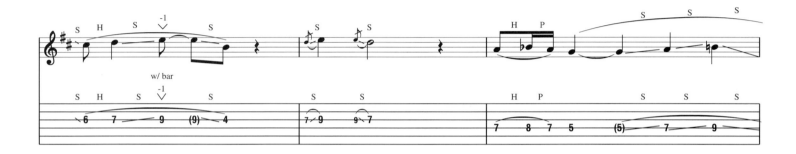

*Point bar at lower strap button and shake between middle and ring finger of right hand.

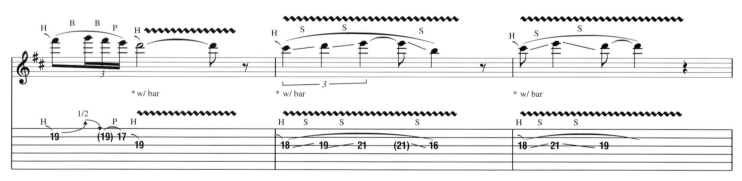

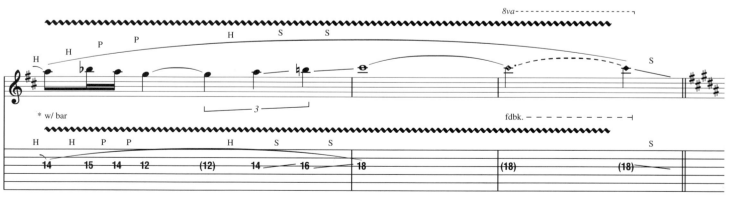

*Key signature denotes E Lydian.

Gtr. 8: w/ Riff A
Gtr. 10 tacet

***Key signature denotes A Mixolydian.

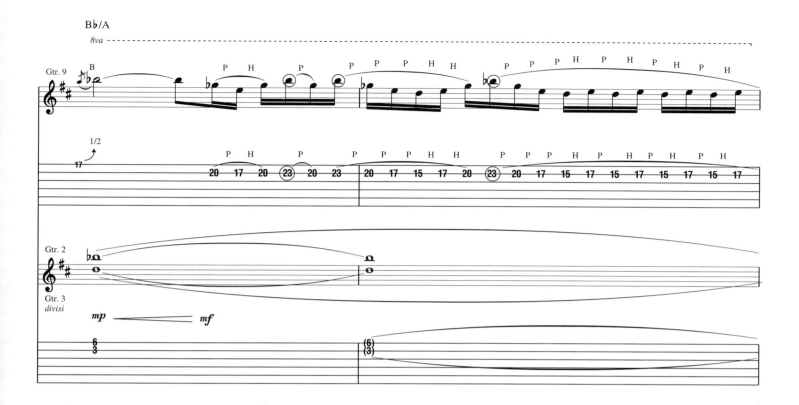

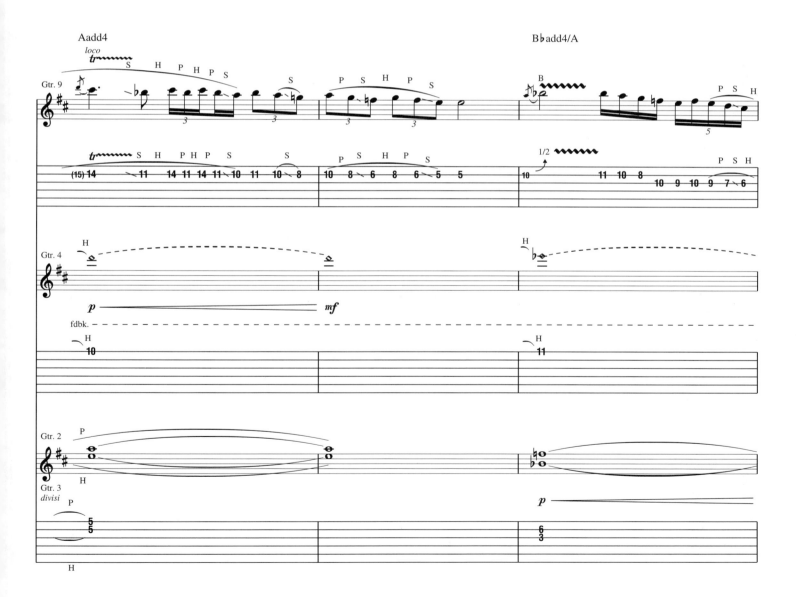

*Key signature denotes E Lydian.

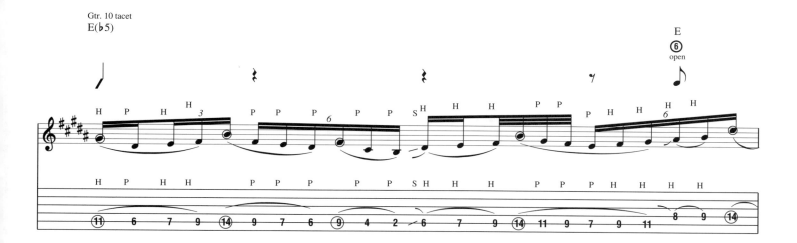

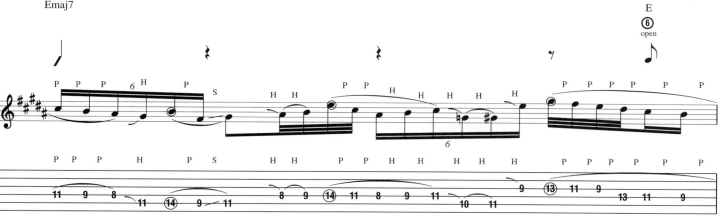

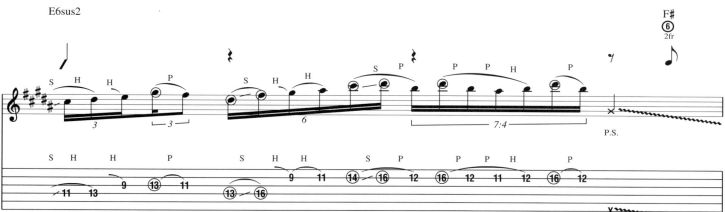

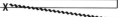

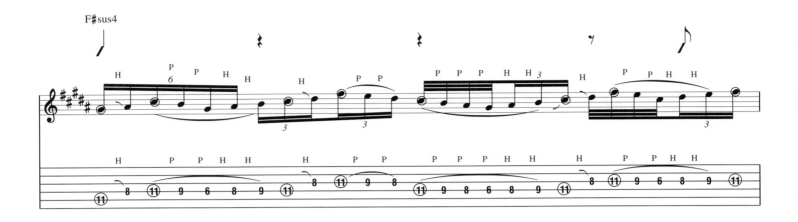

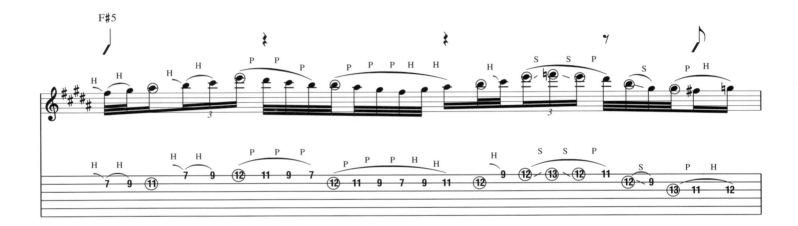

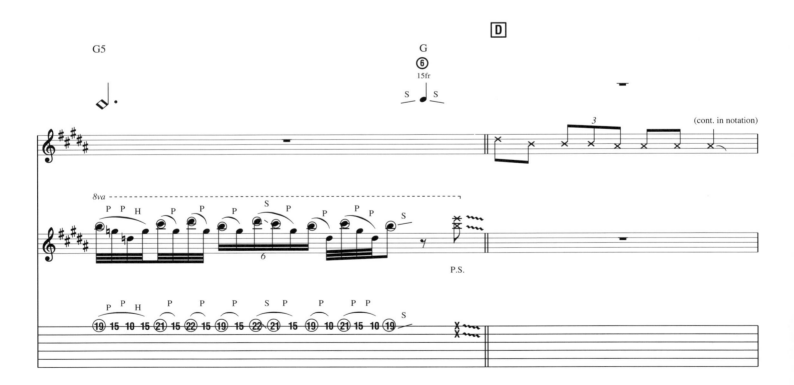

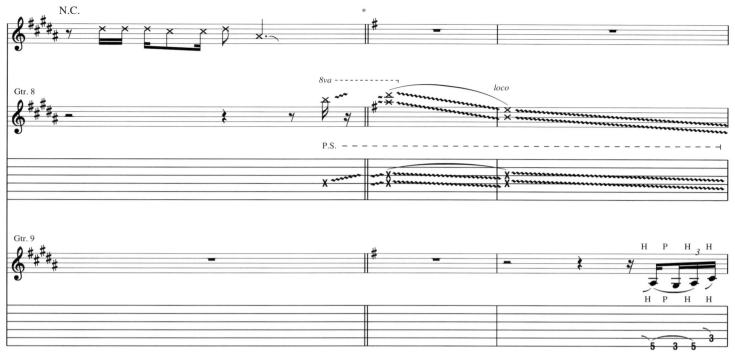

*Key signature denotes A Dorian.

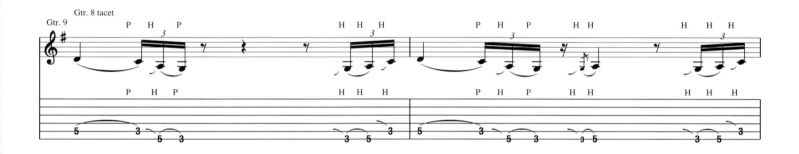

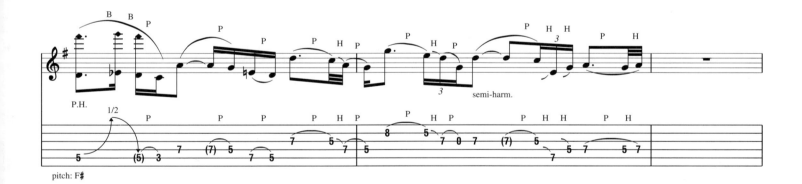

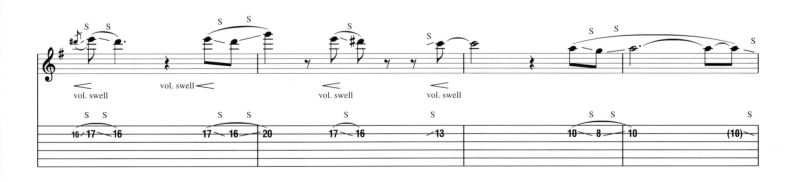

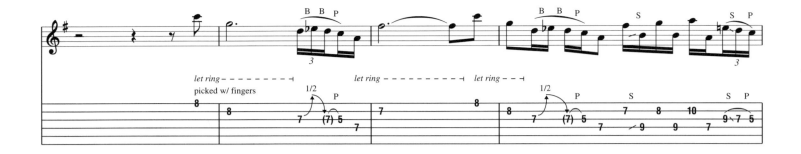

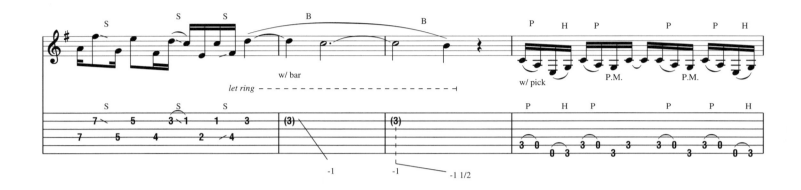

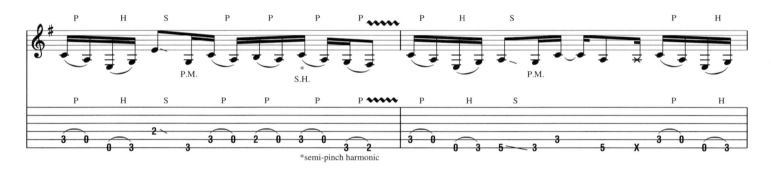

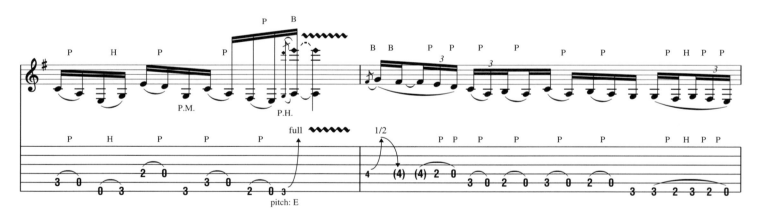

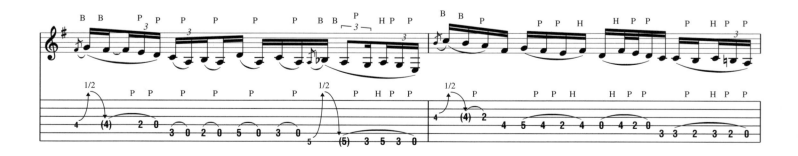

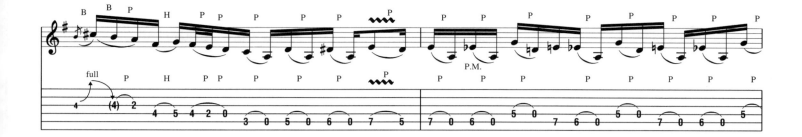

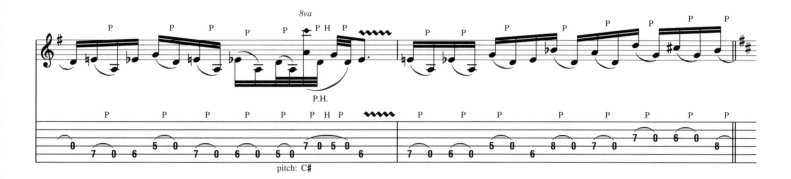

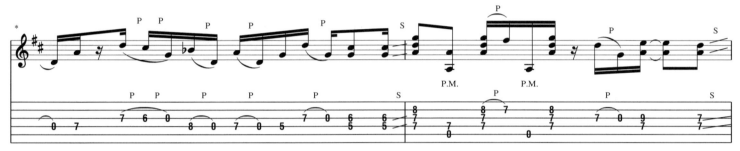

*Key signature denotes A Mixolydian.

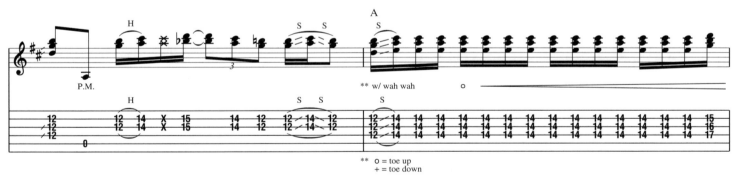

** o = toe up
+ = toe down

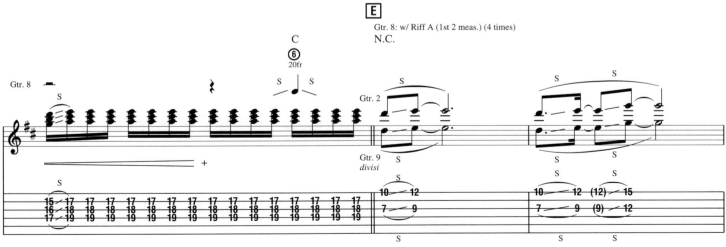

E5   N.C.

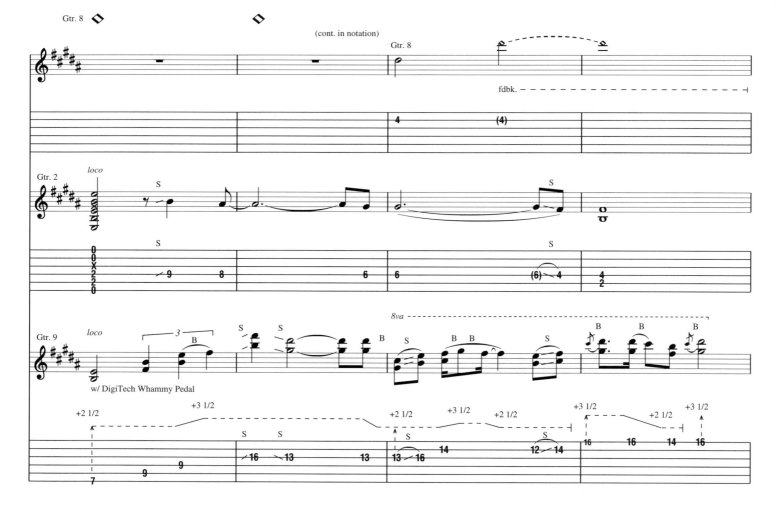

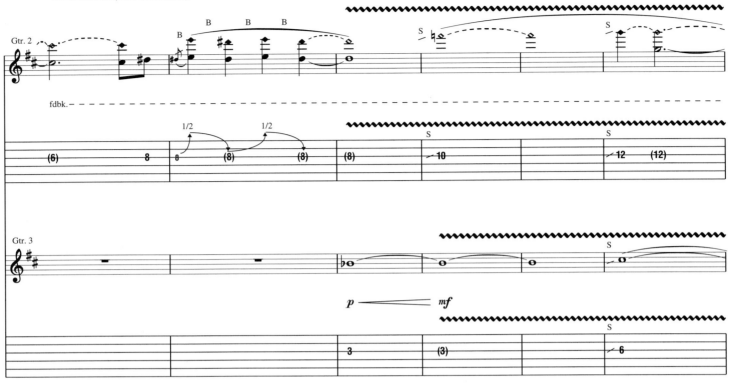

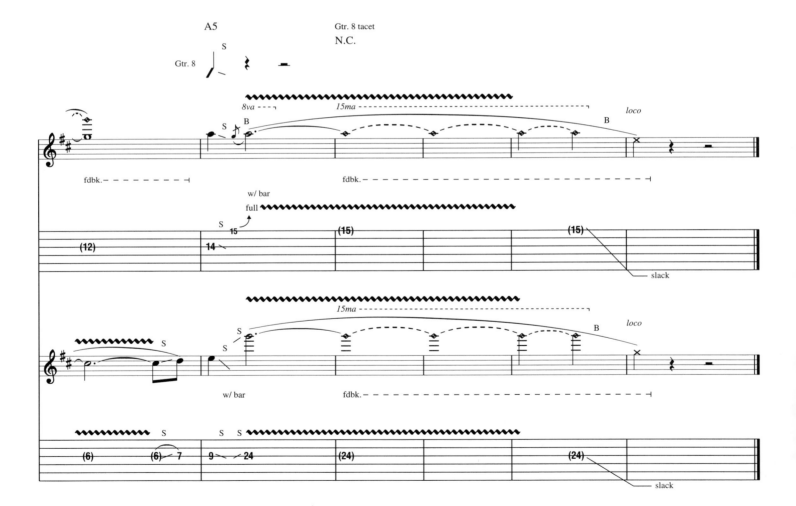

Oooo

By Steve Vai

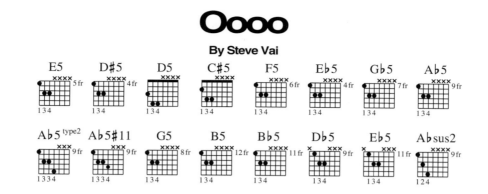

*Key signature denotes C# Dorian.
**7th string tuned to low B.
***Synth. bass arr. for bass gtr.

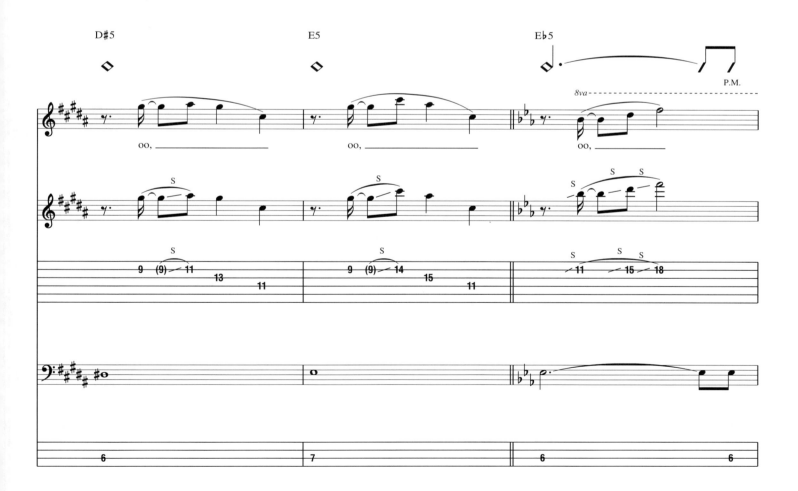

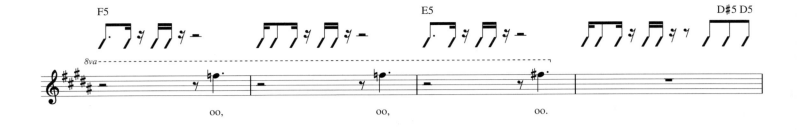

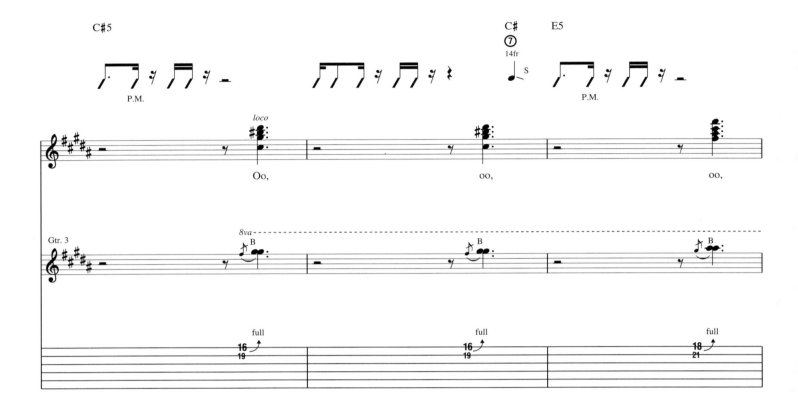

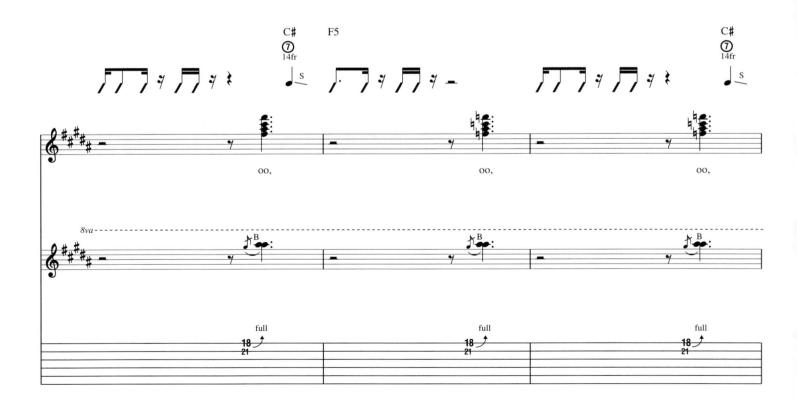

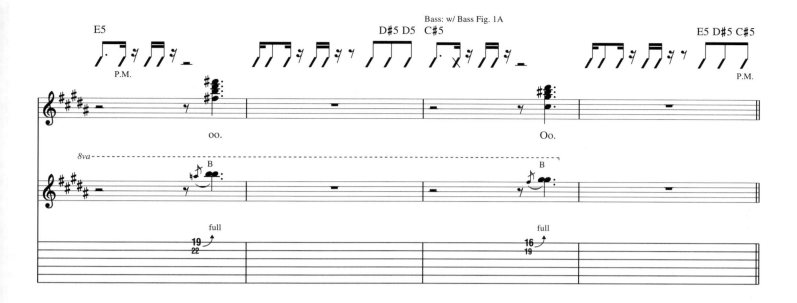

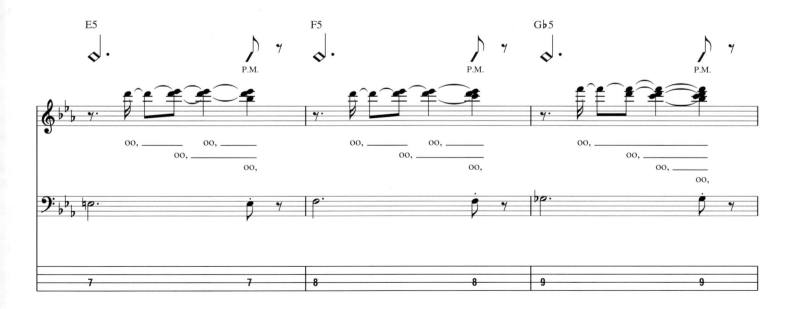

*Keyboards & backwards gtrs. arranged for gtrs.

Gtrs. 1, 2 & 3 tacet

Gtr. 14 tacet

**Gtr. 12 to right of slash in tab.

* w/ harmonizer

*Set to produce pitch an octave above.

H **A Tempo**

Gtrs. 12, 13, & 15 tacet
Bass: w/ Bass Fig. 1 (2 times)
*** A♭/D♭

delay off

***Chord symbols reflect overall harmony.
†Key signature denotes D♭ Lydian.

F#/E

hold bend

††Key signature denotes E Lydian.

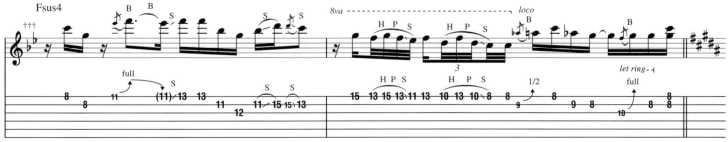

Fsus4

†††Key signature denotes F Mixolydian.

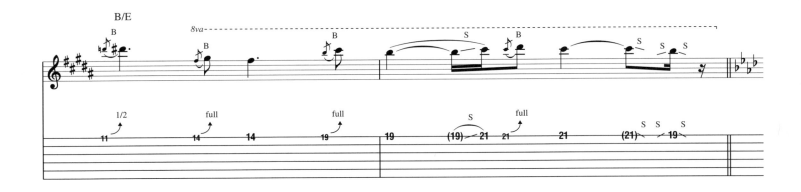

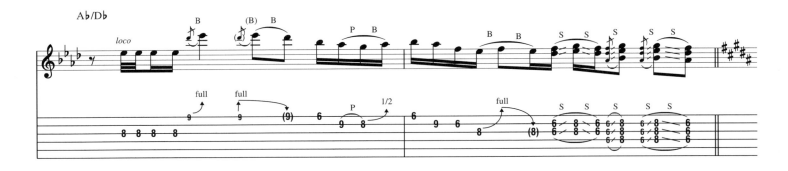

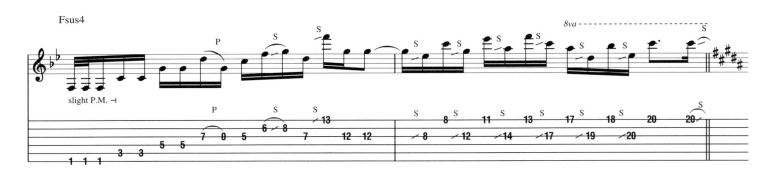

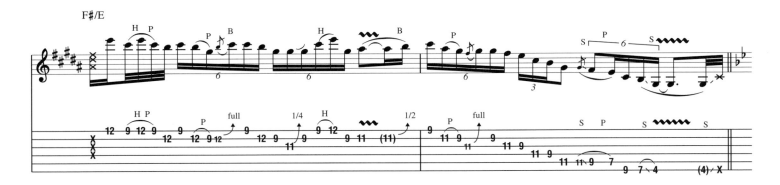

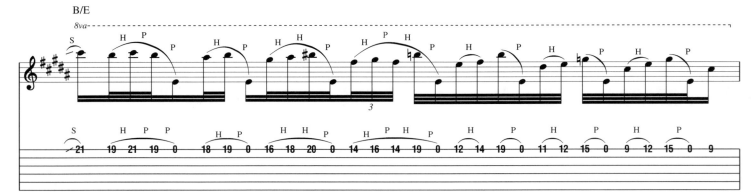

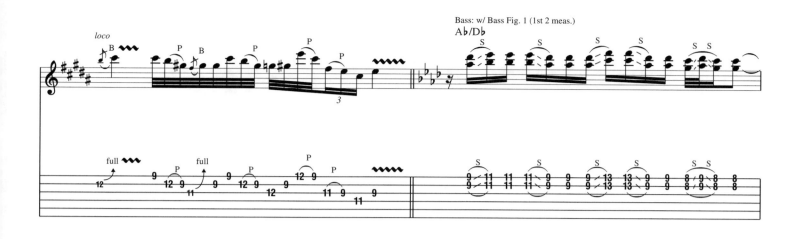

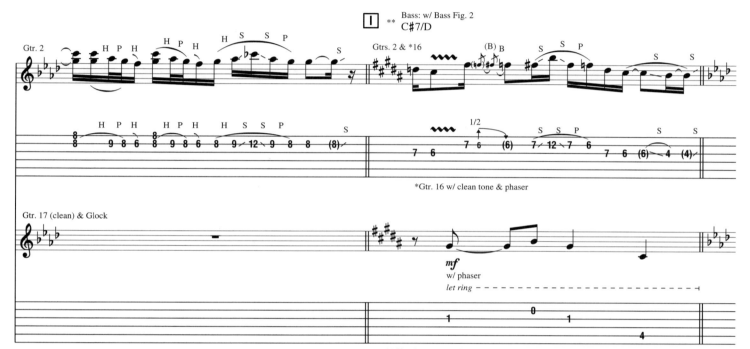

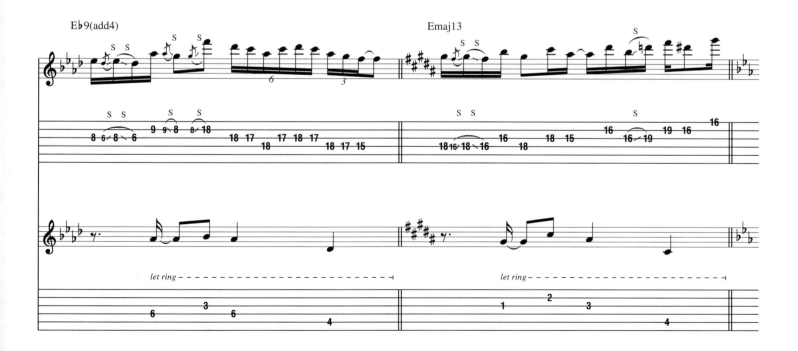

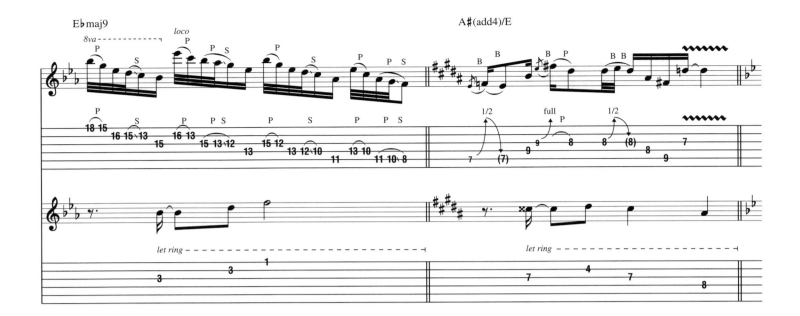

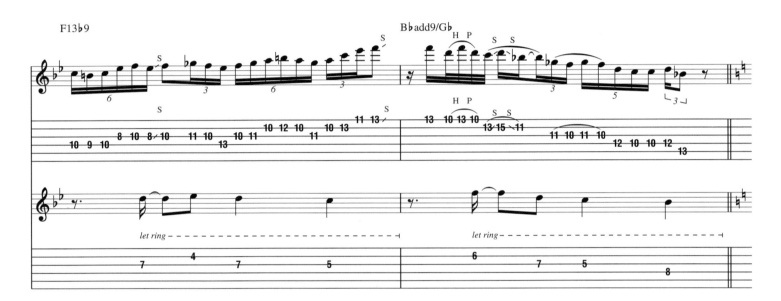

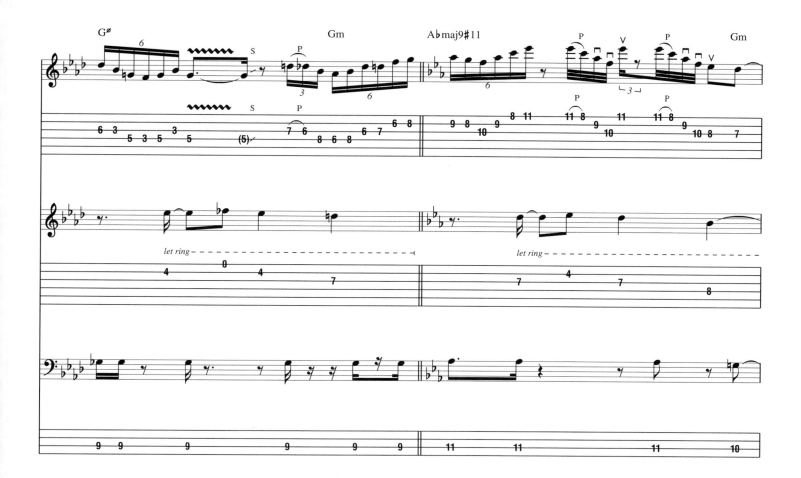

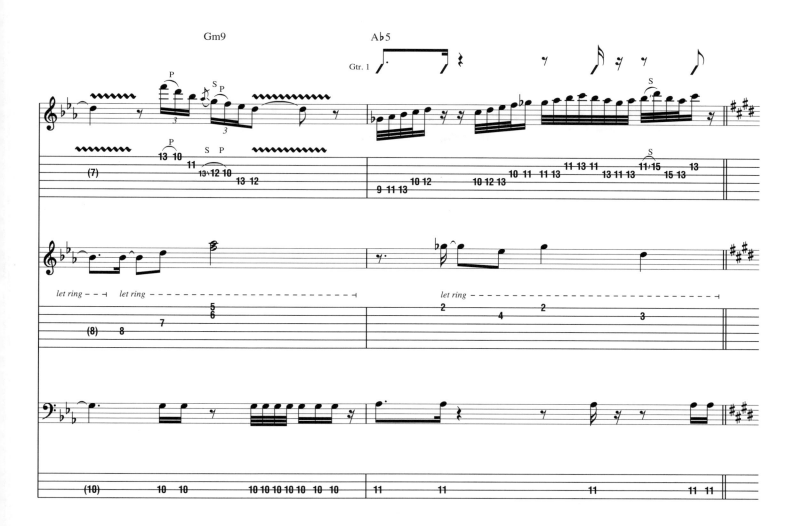

*Right-hand middle finger on 1st string, 1st fret.

54

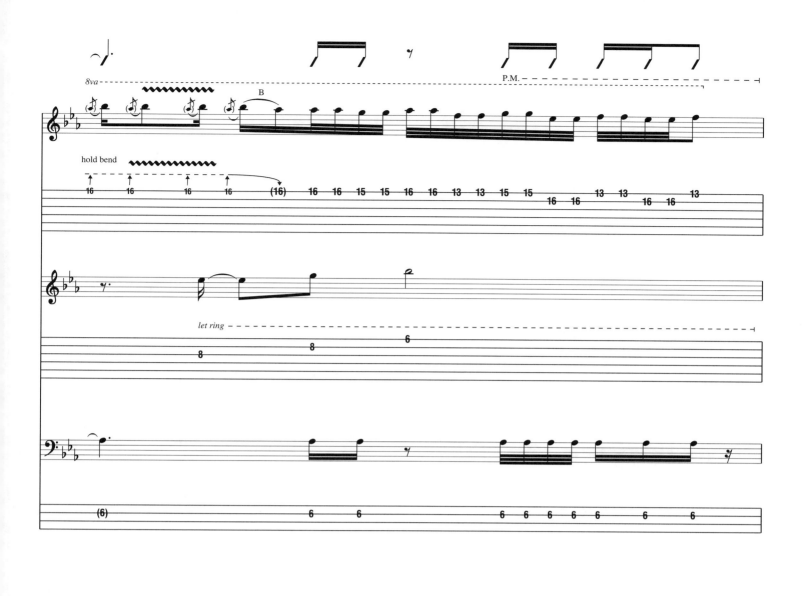

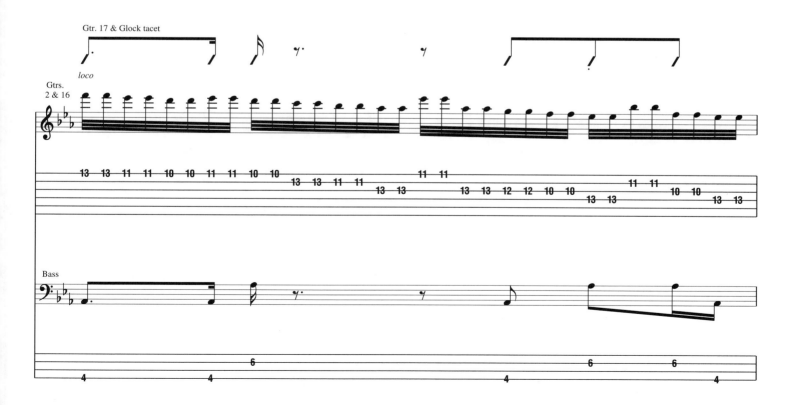

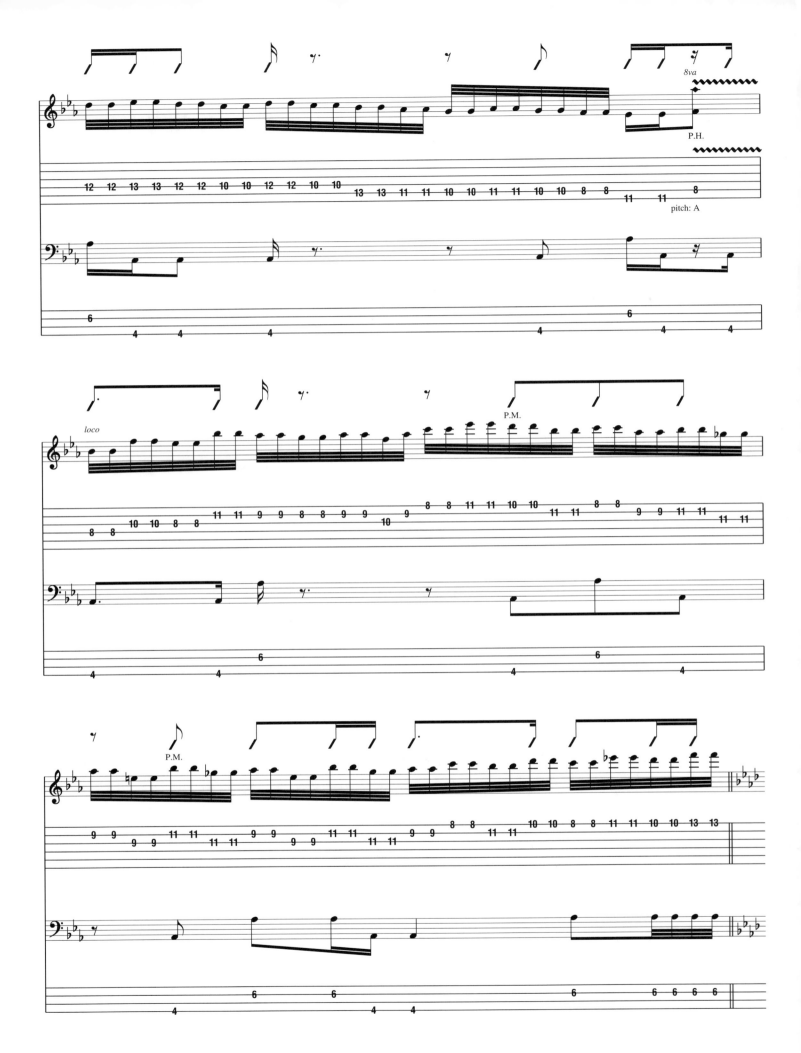

56

Frank

By Steve Vai

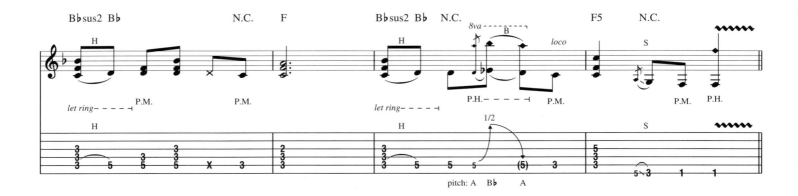

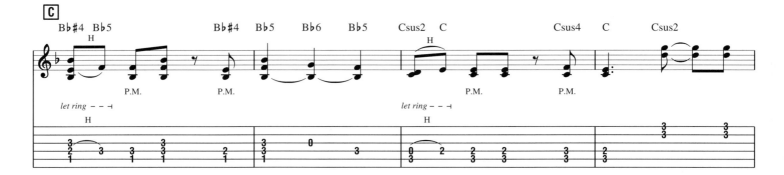

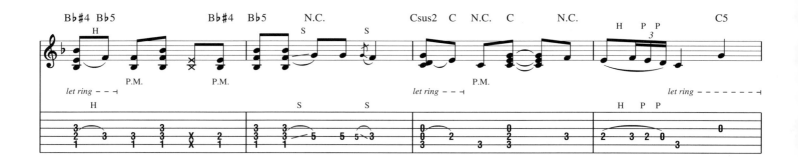

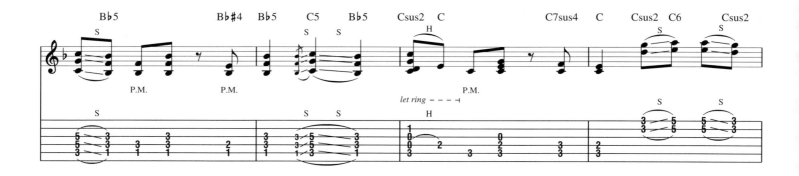

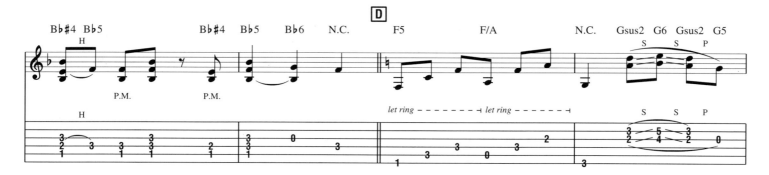

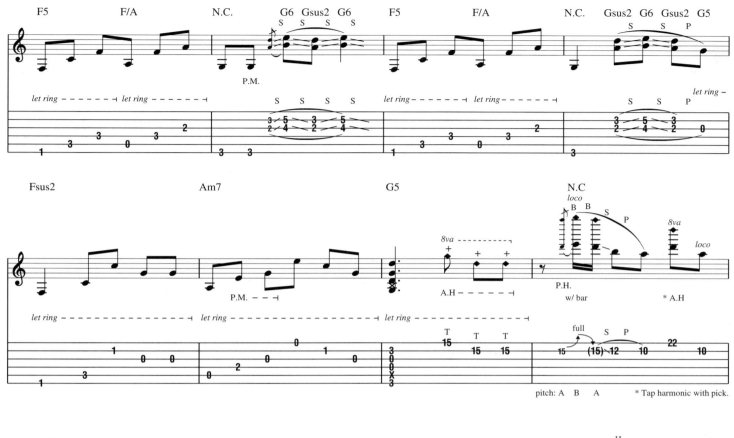

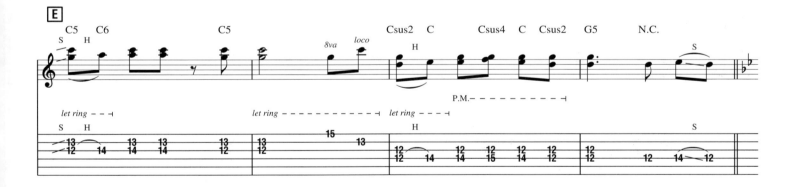

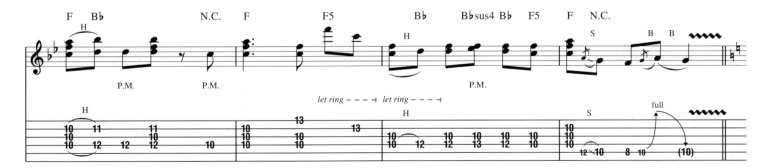

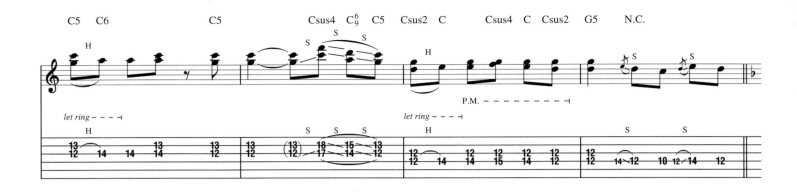

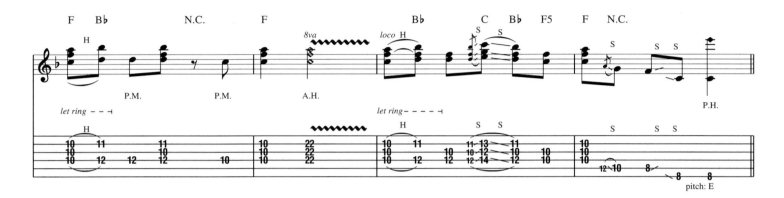

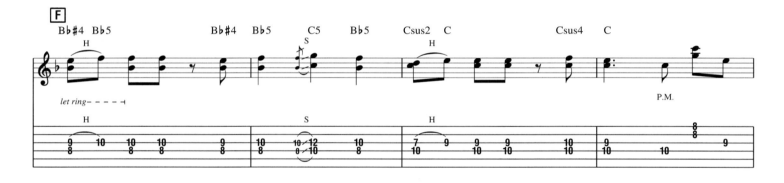

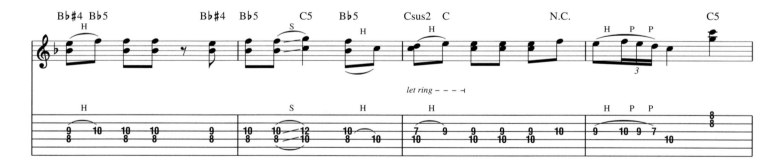

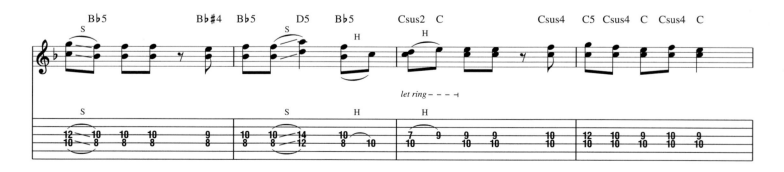

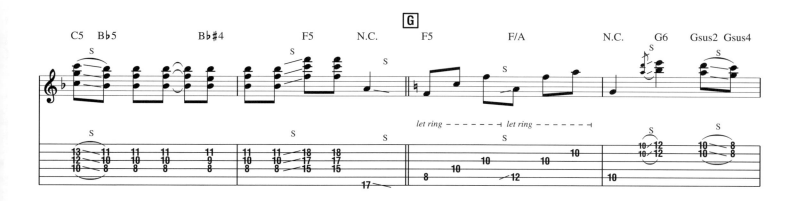

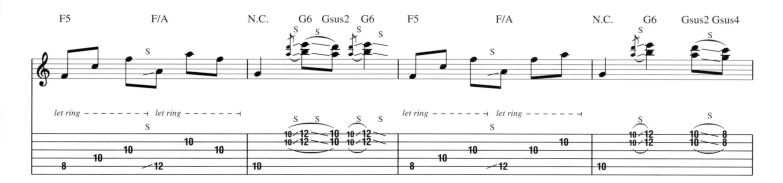

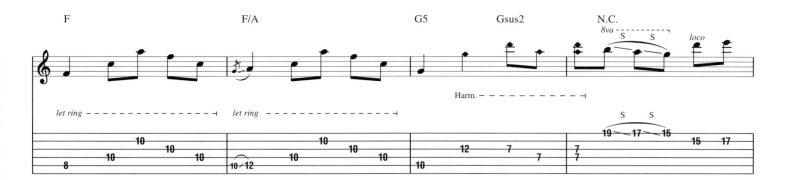

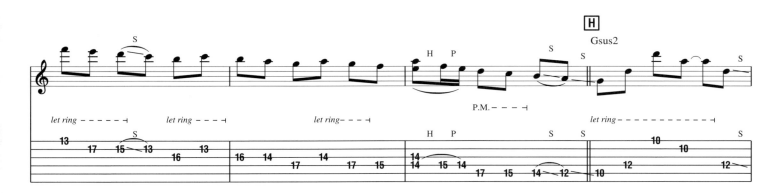

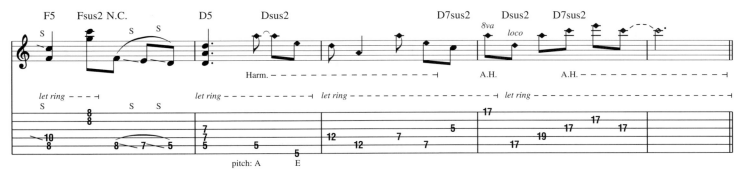

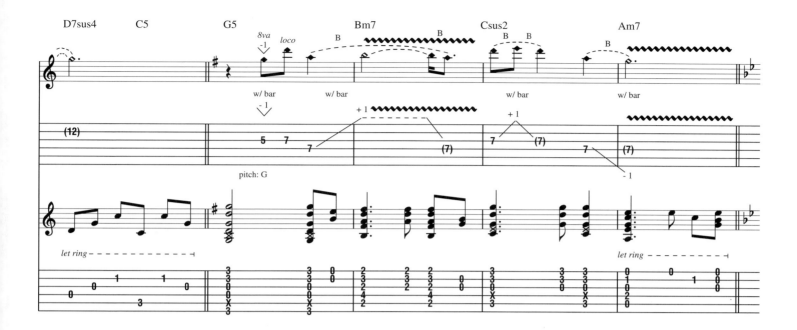

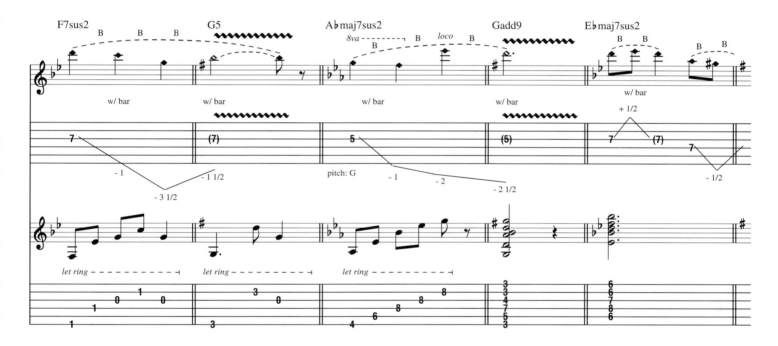

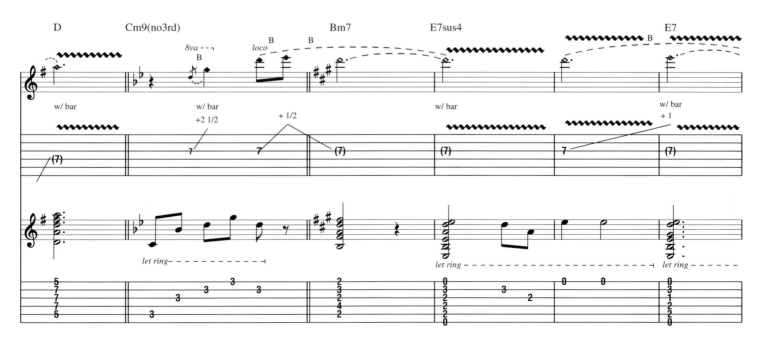

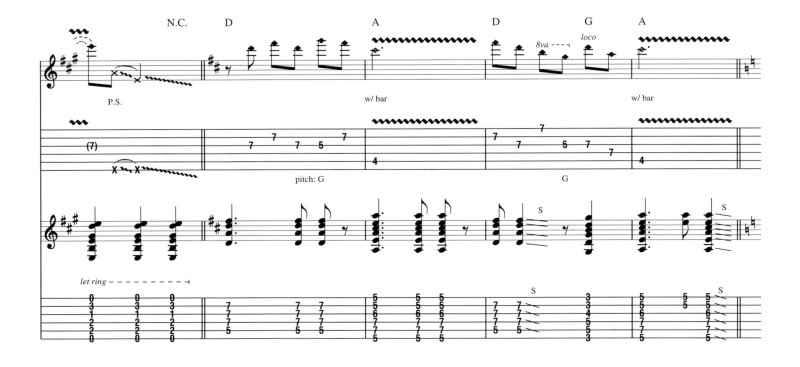

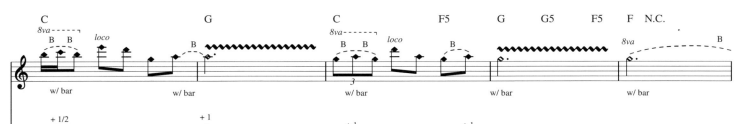

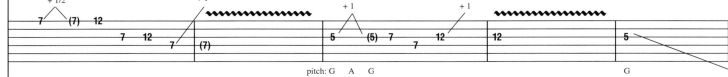

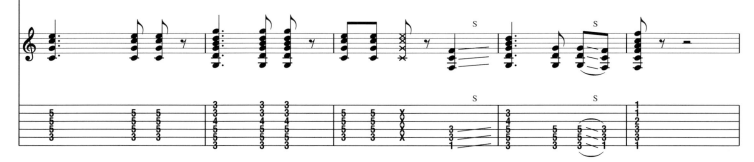

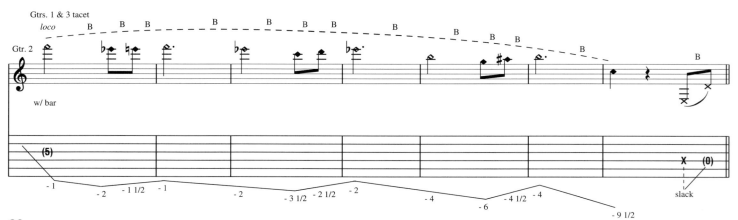

66

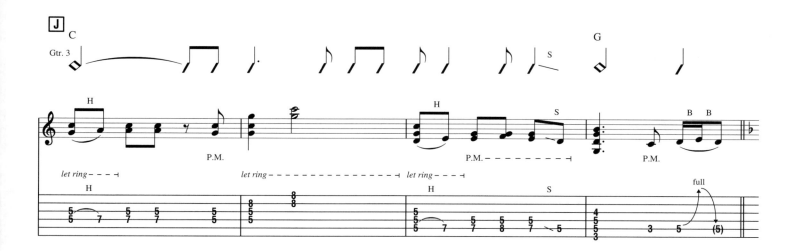

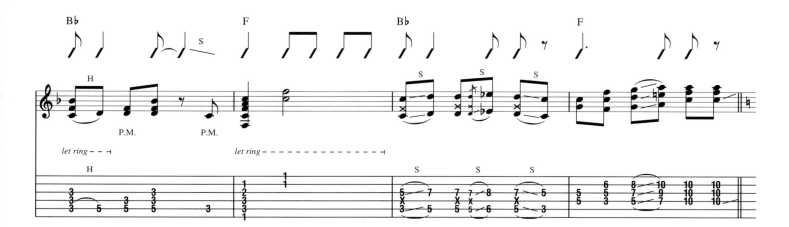

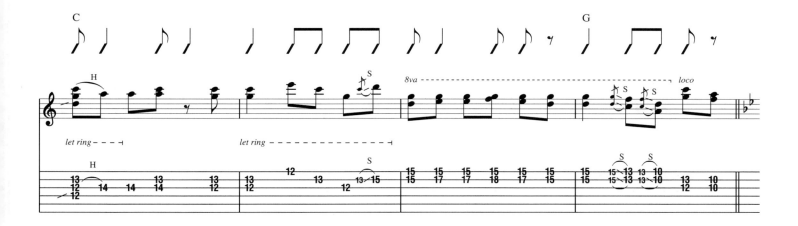

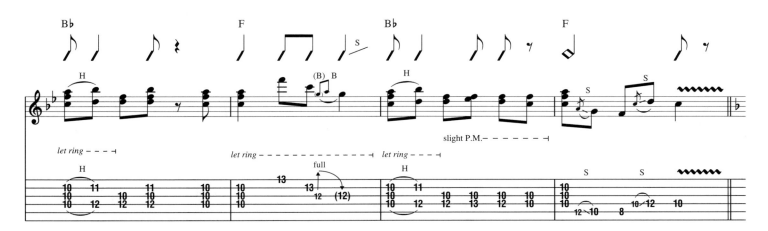

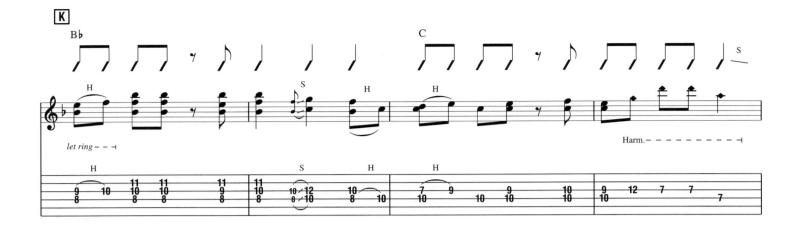

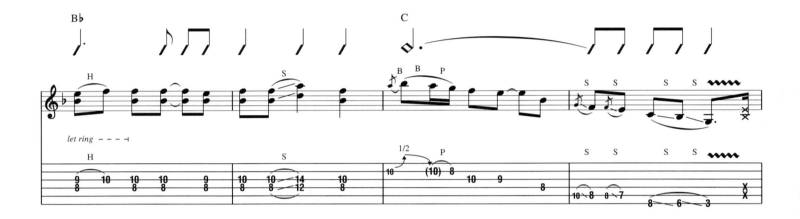

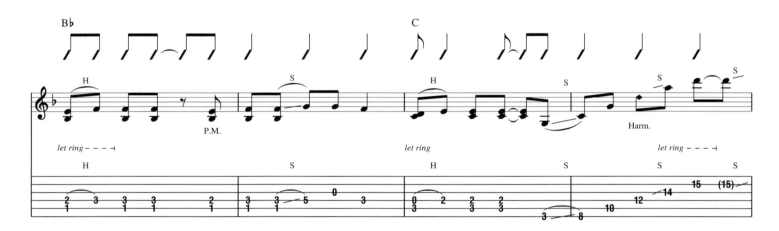

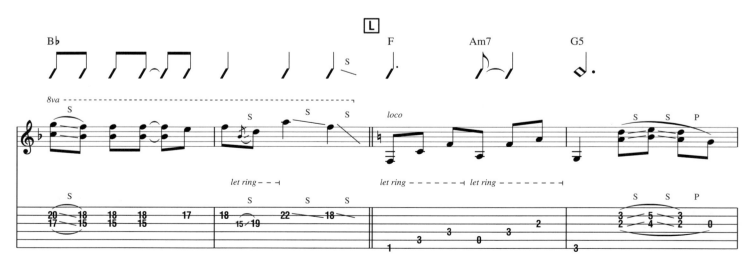

68

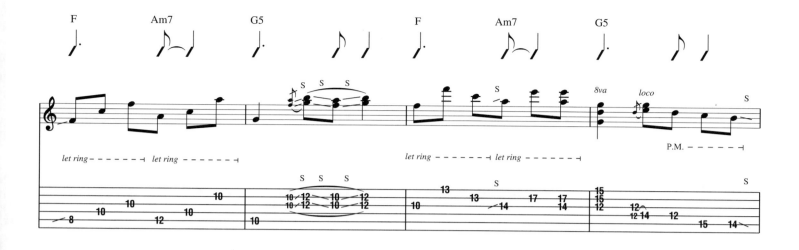

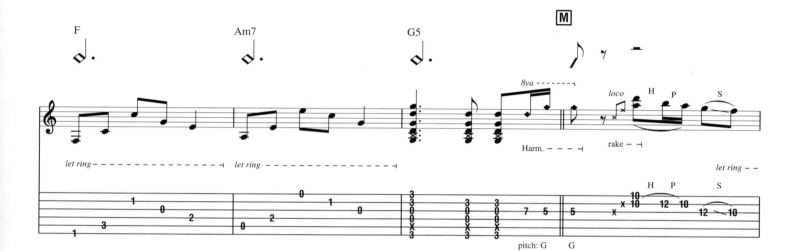

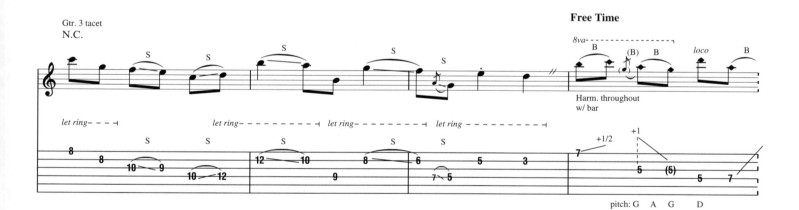

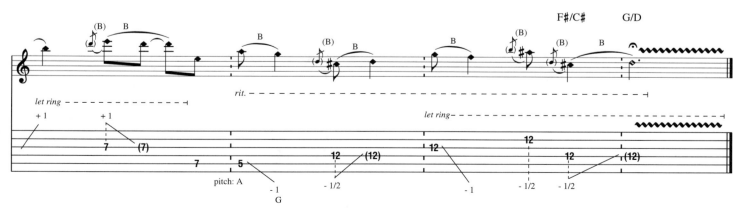

Jibboom

By Steve Vai

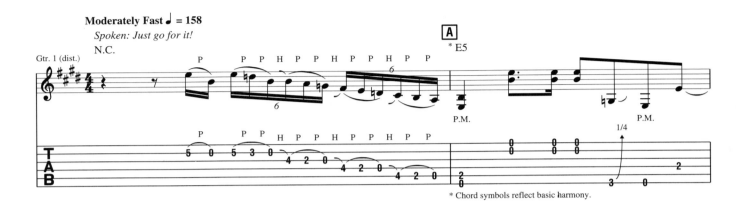

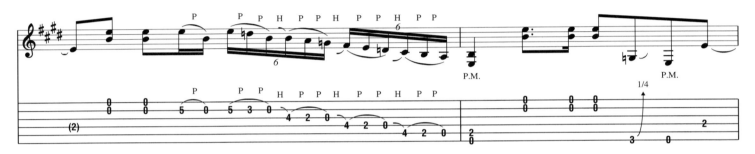

* Chord symbols reflect basic harmony.

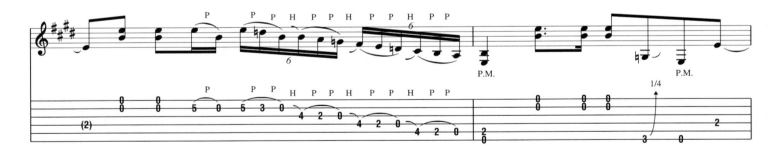

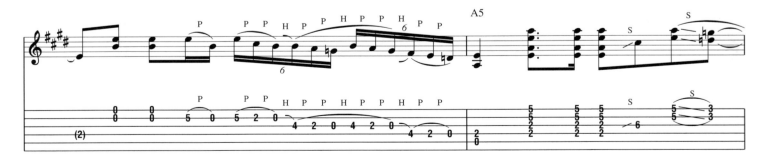

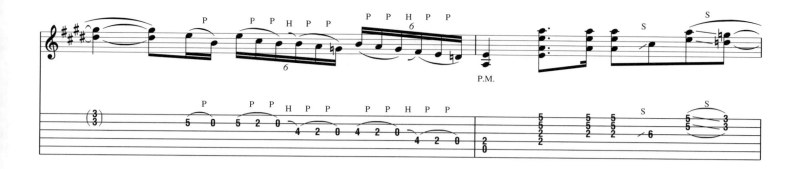

* Lightly touch string to produce random harmonics.

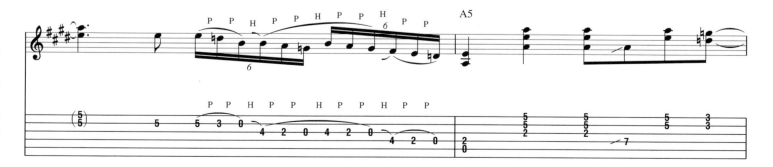

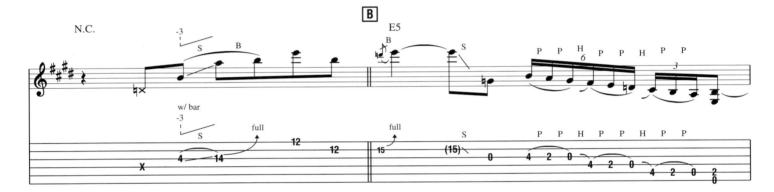

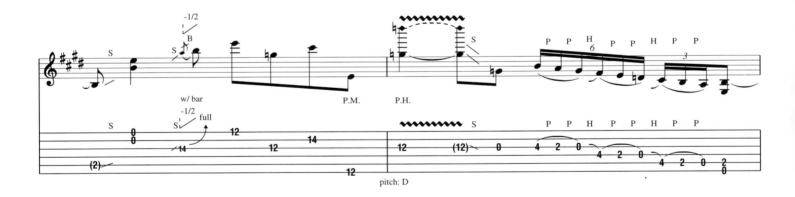

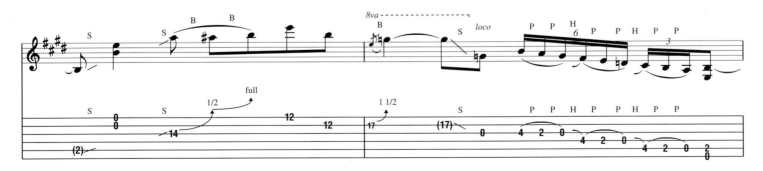

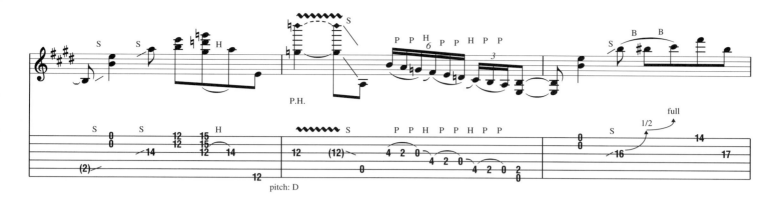

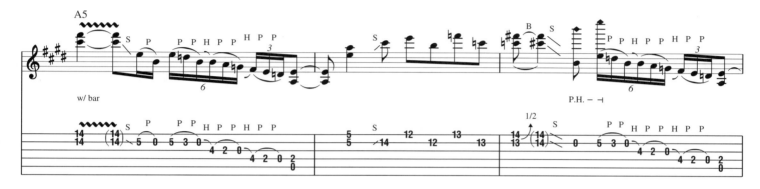

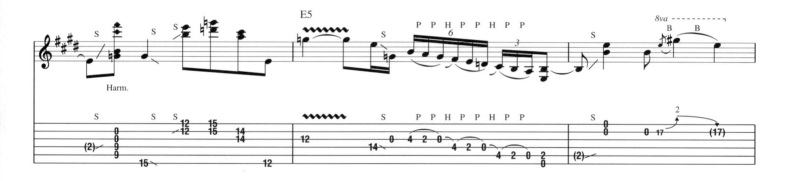

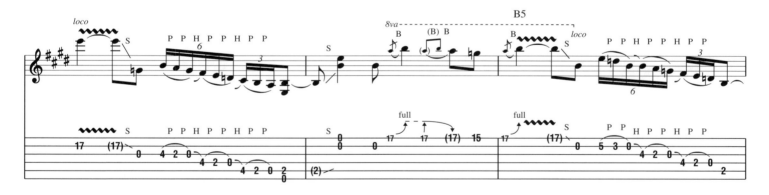

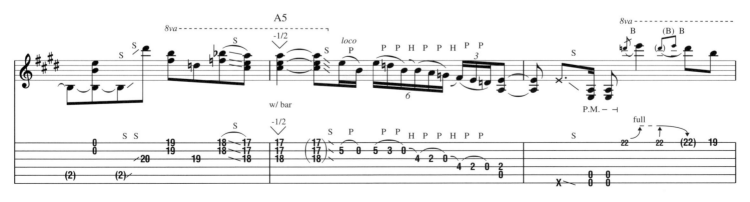

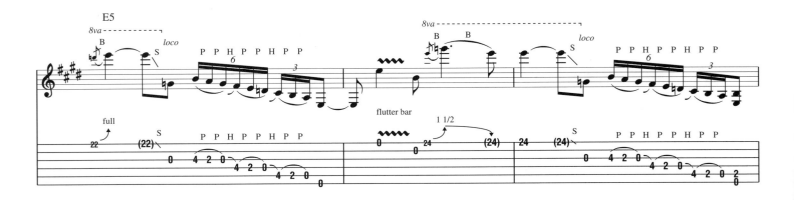

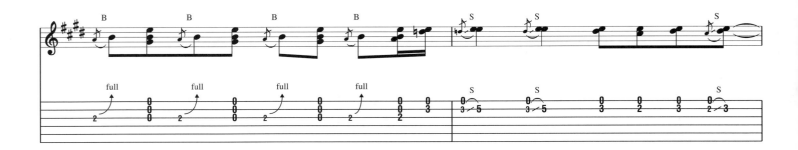

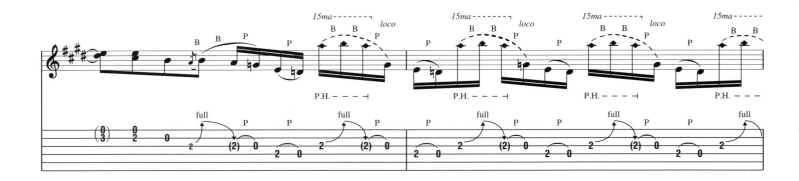

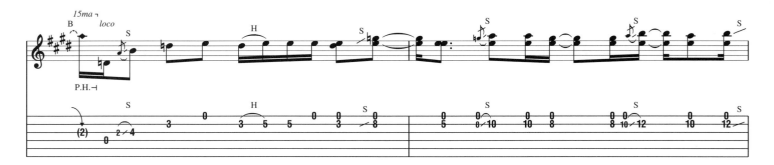

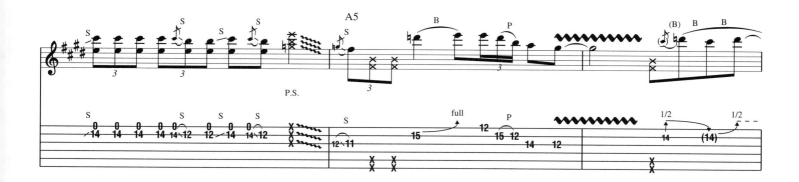

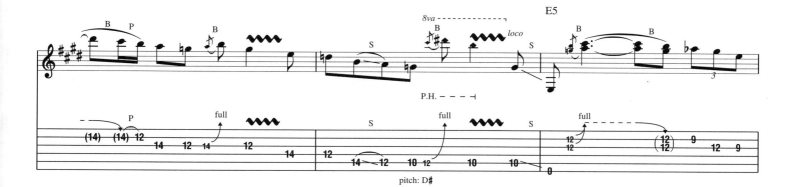

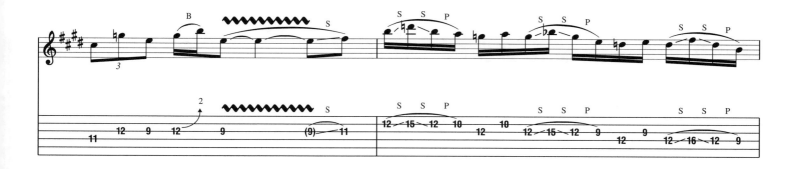

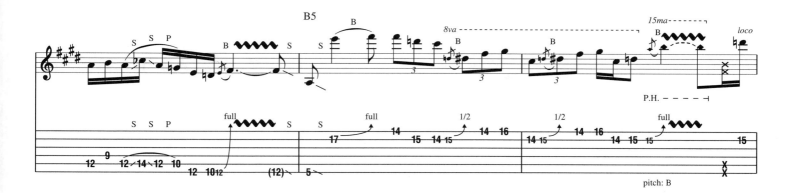

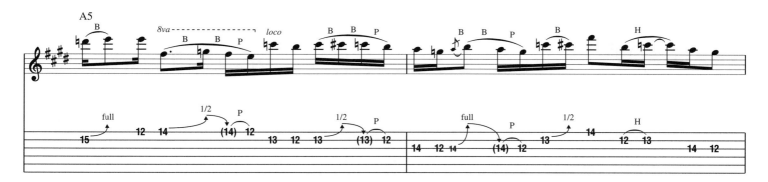

* With bar pointed toward bottom strap button, depress until string "frets out",
  with the higher pitch being fully depressed.

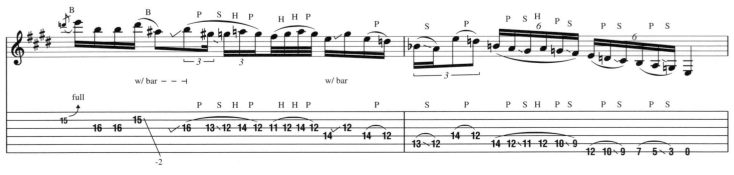

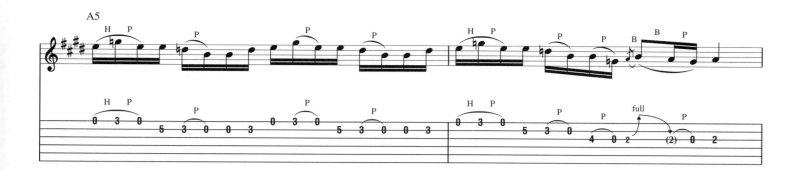

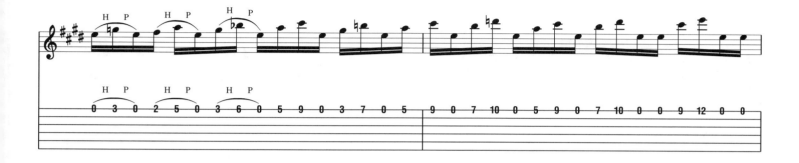

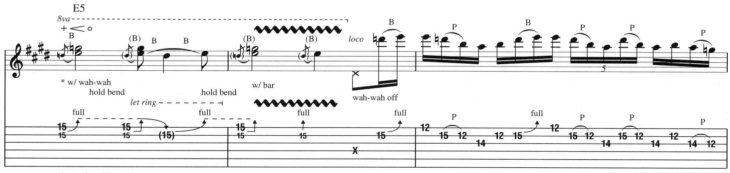

* + = closed (toe up)
o = open (toe down)

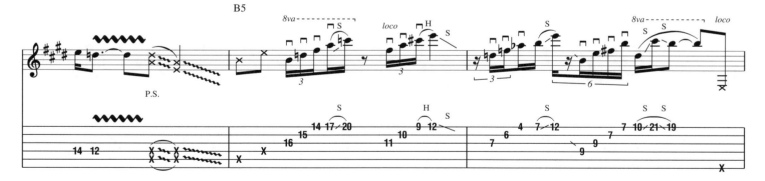

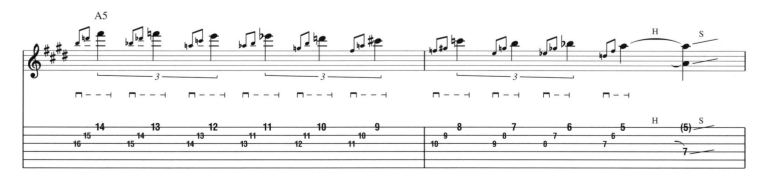

Spoken: Just go for it!

* 2.75 = Just behind the 3rd fret.
2.5 = Halfway between 2nd & 3rd frets.

** T = Thumb on ⑥

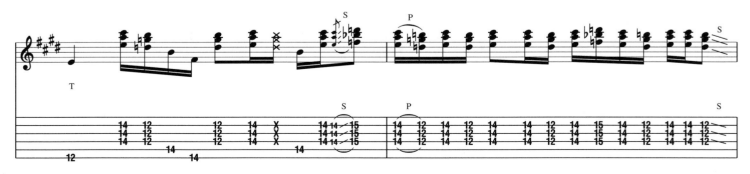

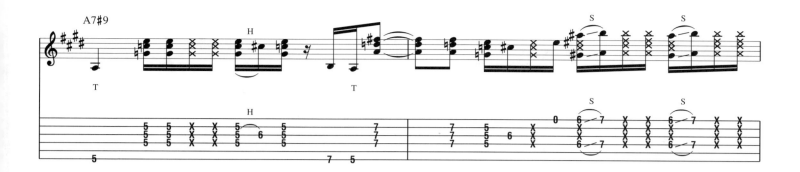

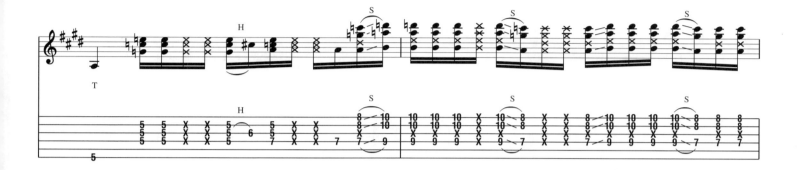

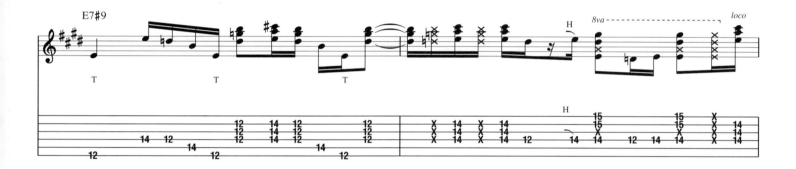

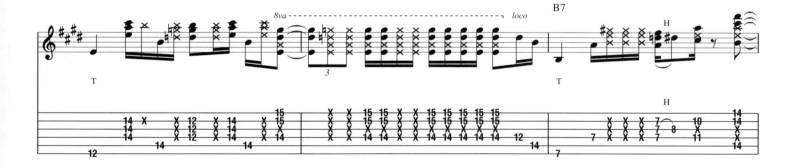

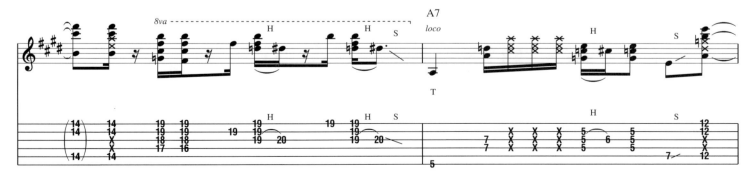

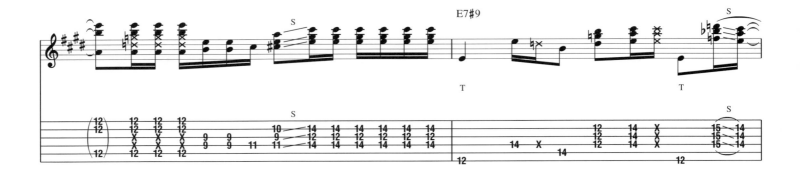

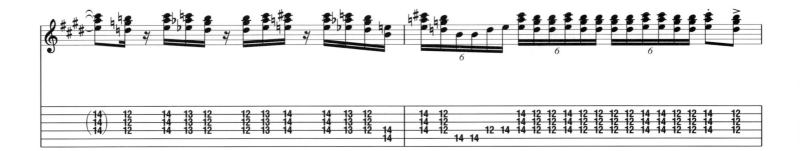

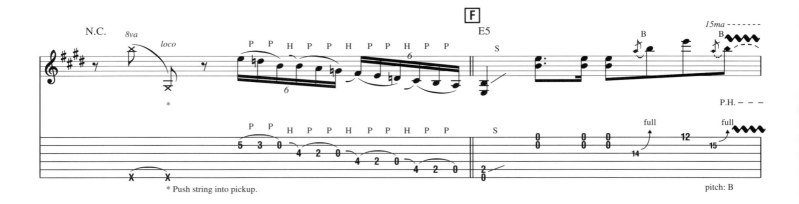

* Push string into pickup.

pitch: B

** Lightly touch string to produce random harmonics.

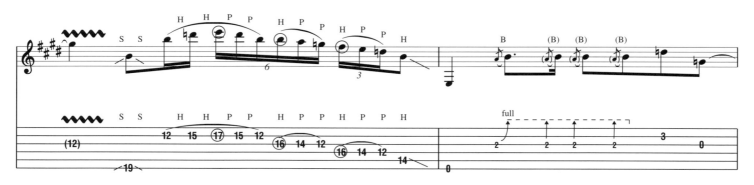

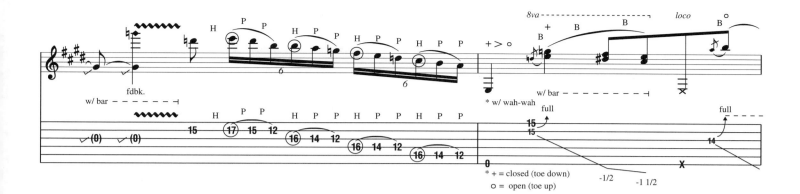

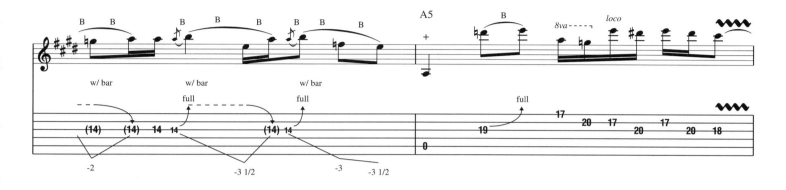

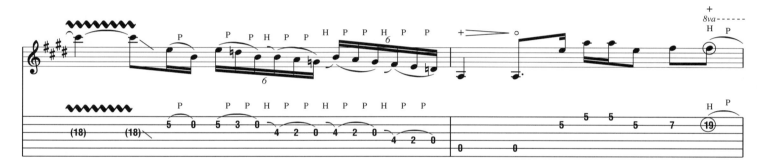

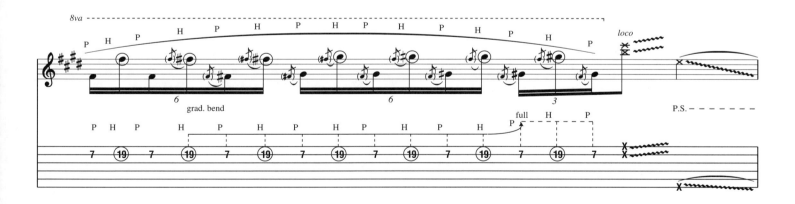

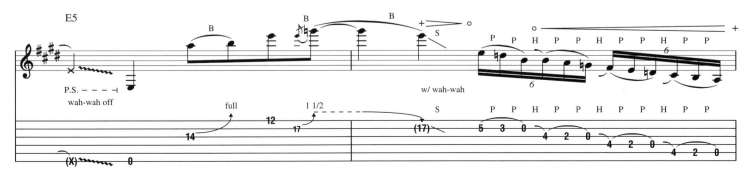

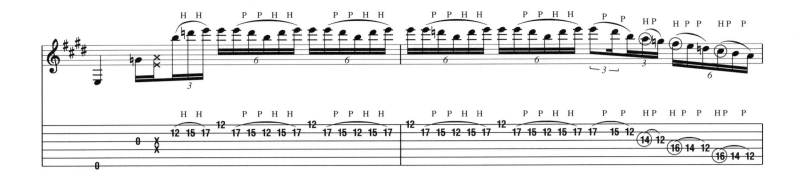

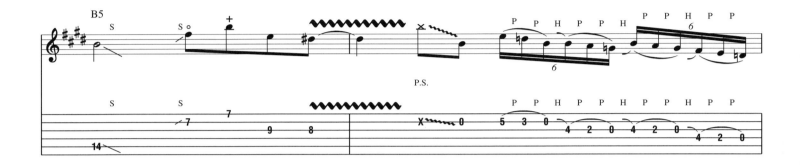

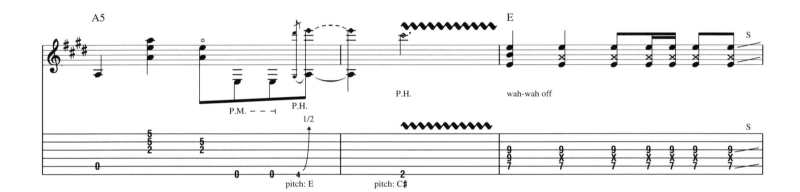

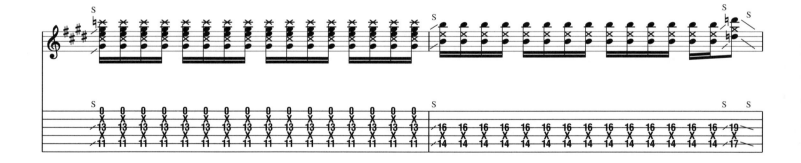

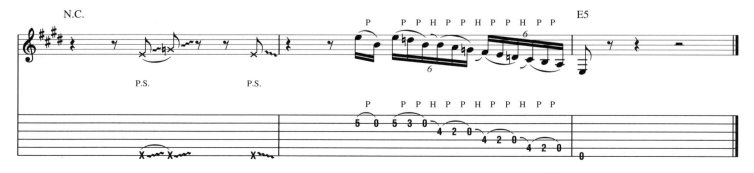

Voodoo Acid

Words and Music by Steve Vai

Melody

Half-Time Feel

*Chord symbols reflect overall harmony.

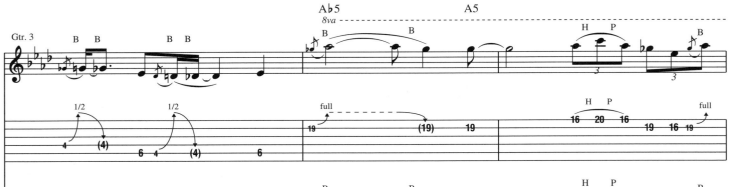

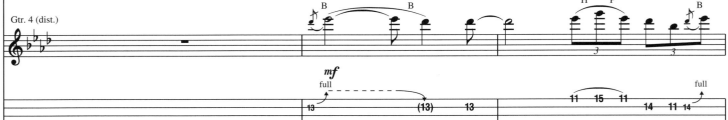

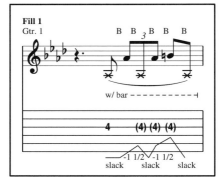

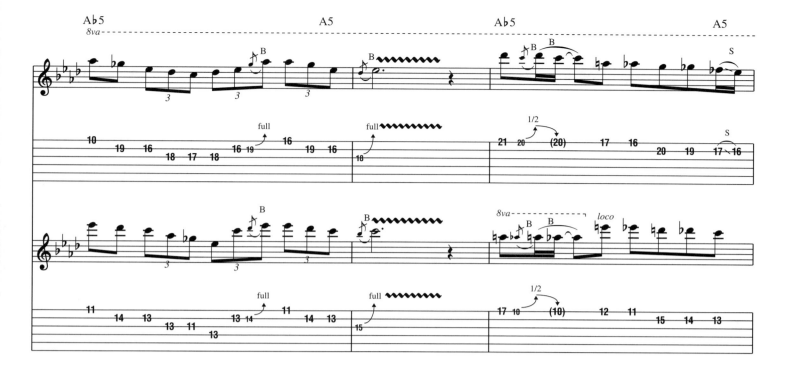

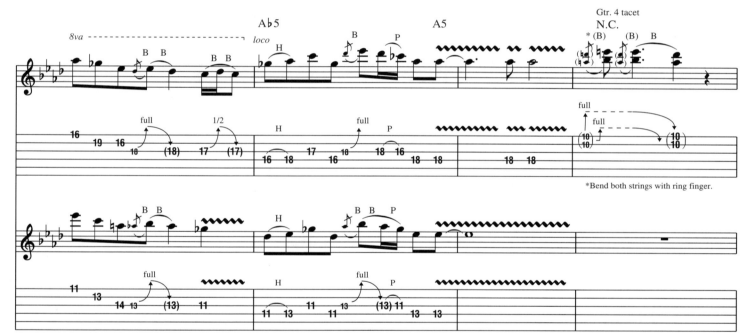

*Bend both strings with ring finger.

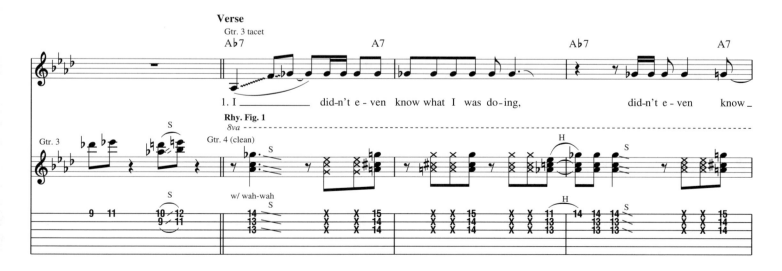

Verse

Gtr. 3 tacet

1. I _____ did-n't e-ven know what I was do-ing, _____ did-n't e-ven know _____

Rhy. Fig. 1

Gtr. 3

Gtr. 4 (clean)

w/ wah-wah

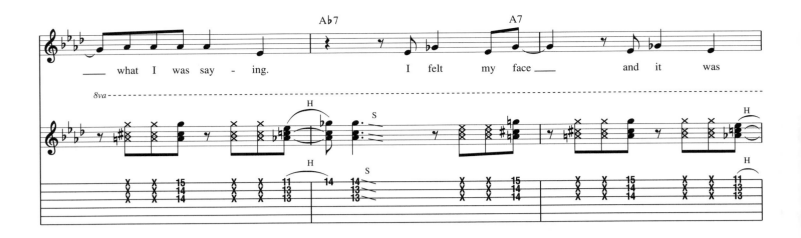

_____ what I was say - ing. I felt my face _____ and it was

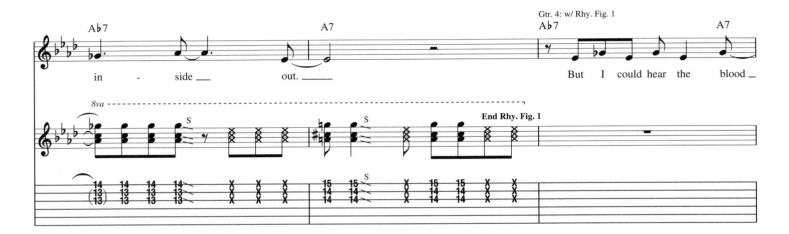

in - side _____ out. _____ But I could hear the blood _____

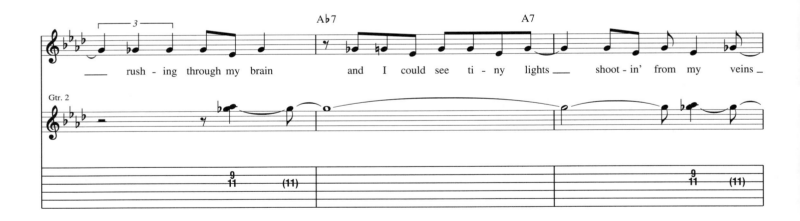

_____ rush - ing through my brain and I could see ti - ny lights _____ shoot - in' from my veins _____

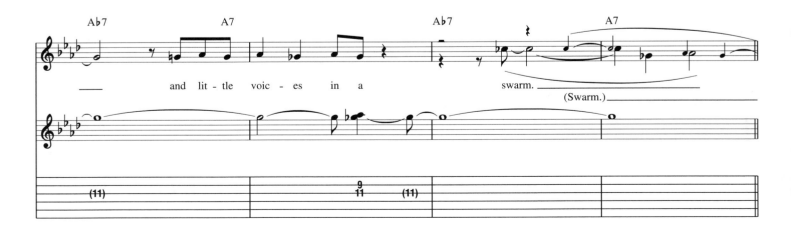

_____ and lit - tle voic - es in a swarm. _____
(Swarm.) _____

Guitar Solo

Gtr. 2 tacet
Bass: w/ Bass Fig. 1 (4 times)

Oh, you go, boy! ___

Dance!!! ___

w/ ad lib humming & moaning, next 10 meas.

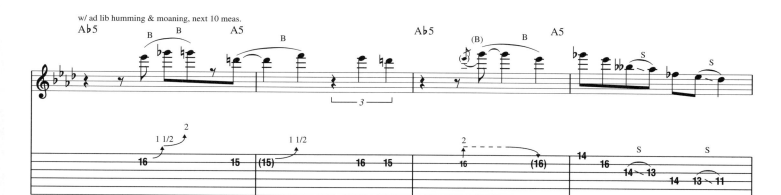

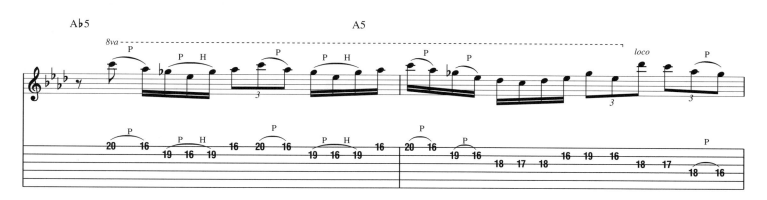

And then that feel-ing you al-ways get, ___ well, it made me make a mess, and I ___ was left ___ in a pud-dle ___

Free Time

Ab5   N.C.

___ of, mm, ___ mm,... ___ *(gurgling)* hon - ey.

A Tempo
(Sound effect, drums)

Guitar Solo
Bass: w/ Bass Fig. 1 (12 times)
Gtr. 2: w/ Fill 4

* w/ DigiTech Whammy Pedal
w/ bar
steady gliss.

*o = open (toe up): set to harmonize a 4th higher;
+ = closed (toe down): set to harmonize a 5th higher

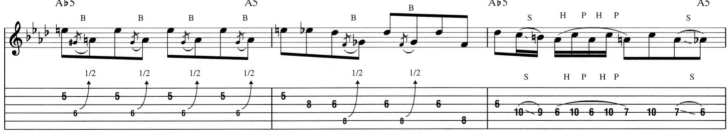

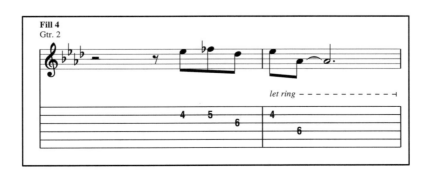

Fill 4
Gtr. 2

let ring - - - - - - - - - -

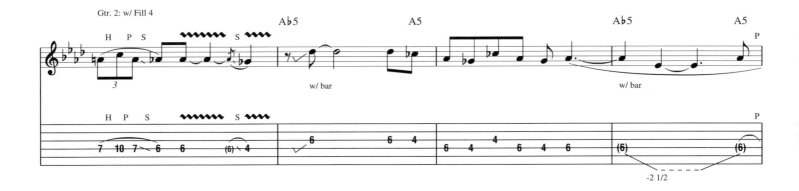

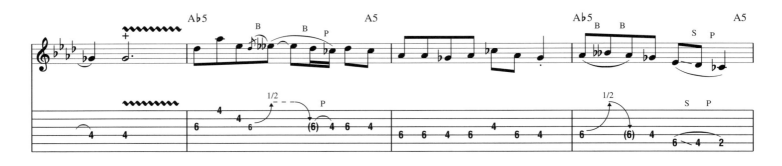

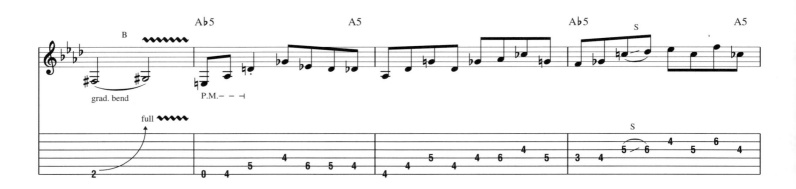

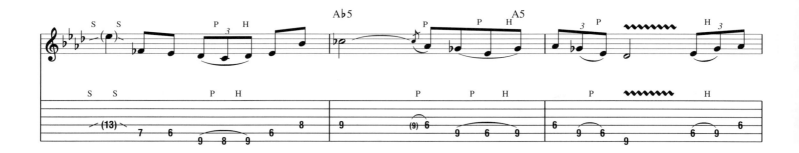

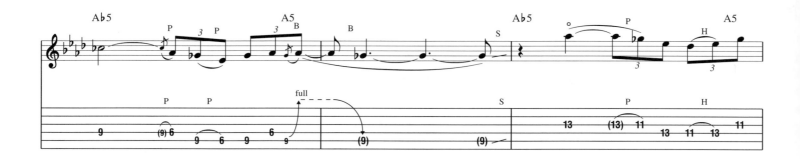

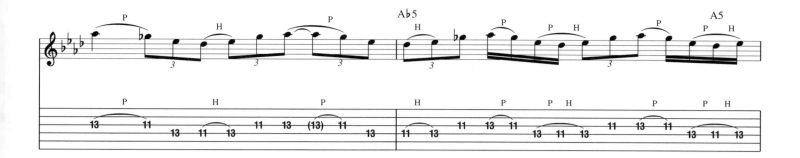

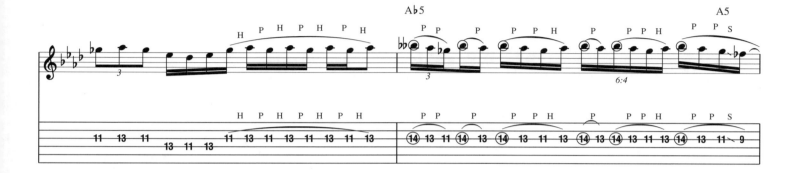

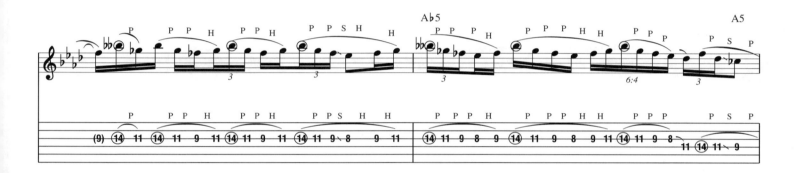

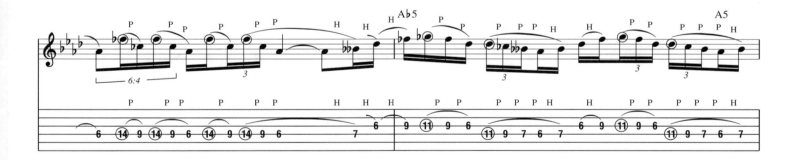

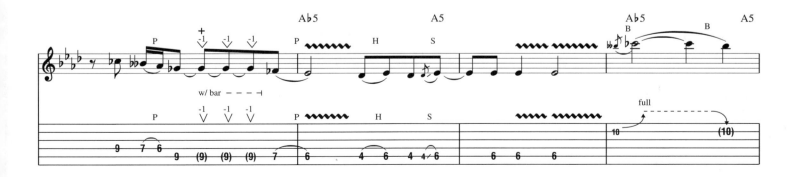

94

Verse

5. When I a - woke, __ I thought I died. __ I ac - tu - al - ly did, __ but not in -

side. (I) lay there swim - ming in a pool of scum and smut __ that my e - go threw up.

Now I walk on wa - ter. Now I see the light. __

And if you see my friend, the Queen, __ then you'll be all right. __

*w/ DigiTech Whammy Pedal
flutter bar

*Set to shift pitch an octave higher when depressed.

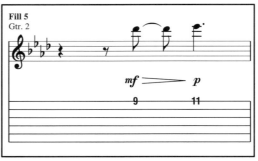

96

Outro-Guitar Solo

Bass: w/ Bass Fig. 1 (13 times)

Windows to the Soul

By Steve Vai

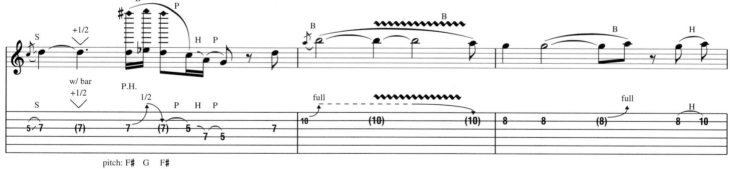

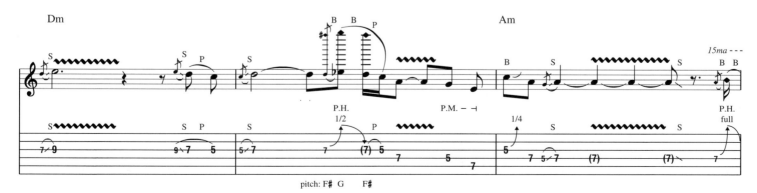

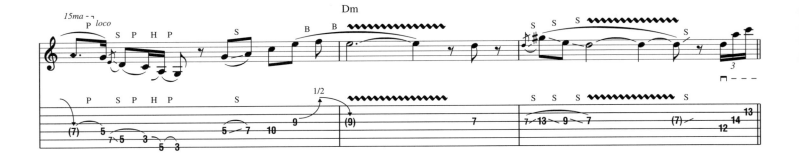

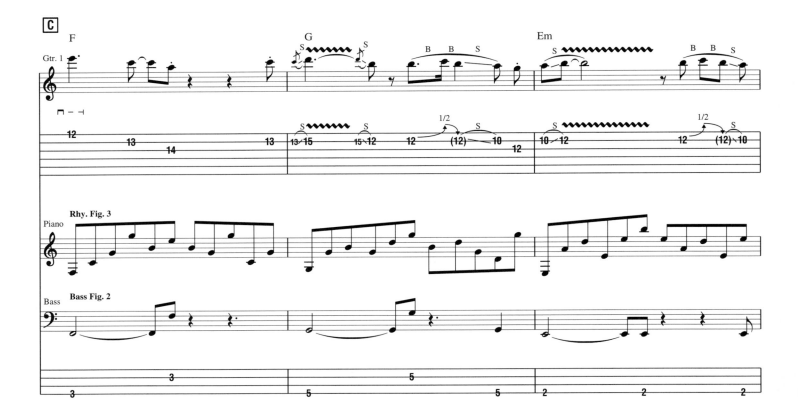

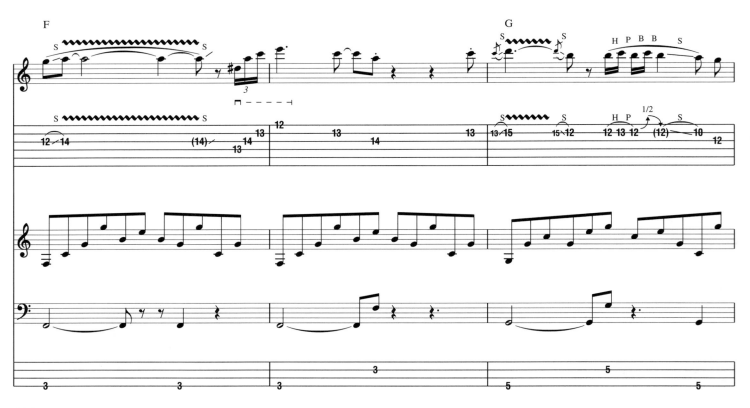

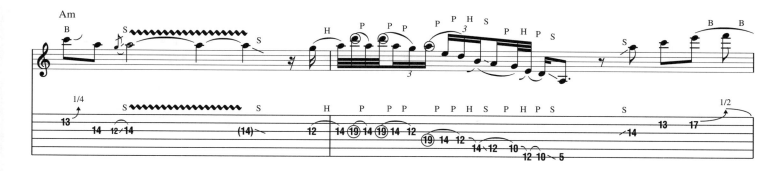

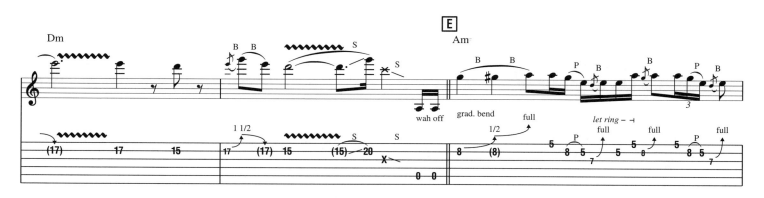

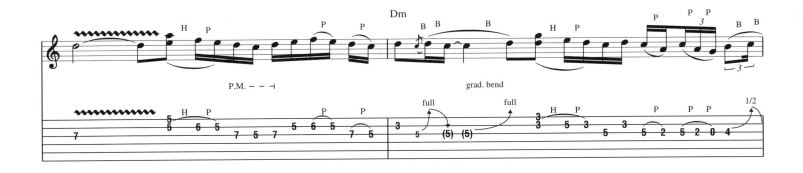

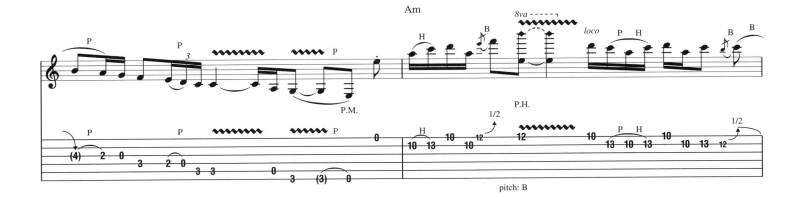

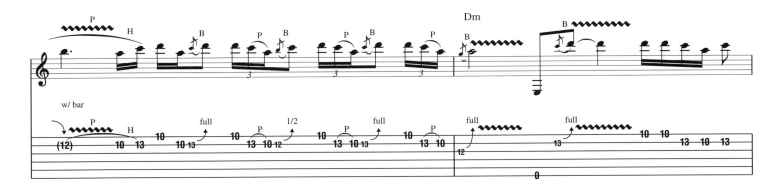

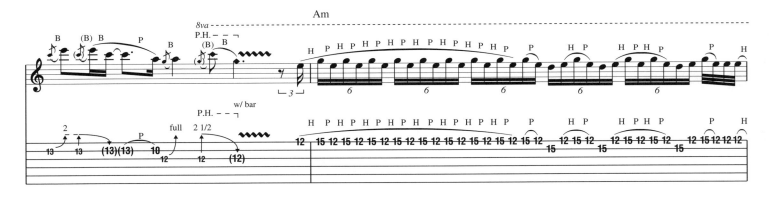

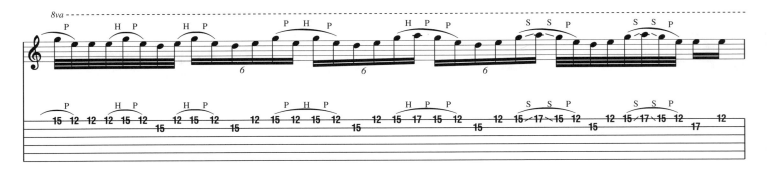

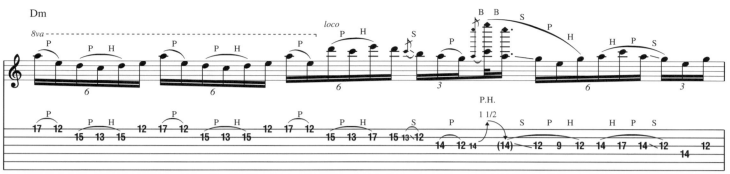

pitch: E G   E

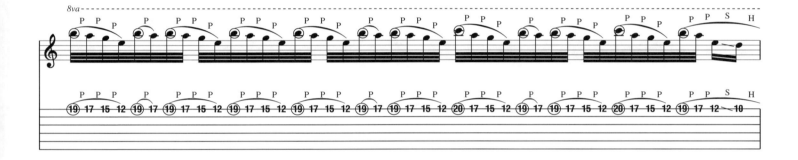

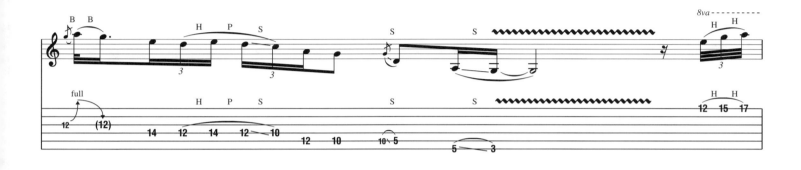

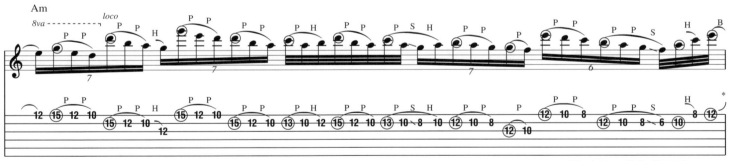

* Bend string w/ L.H., till end of next meas.

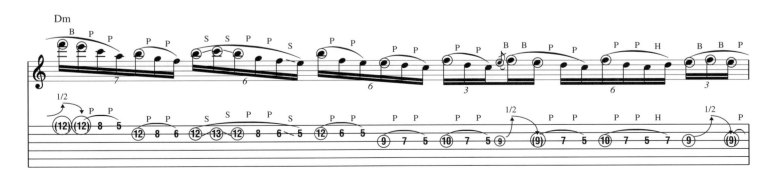

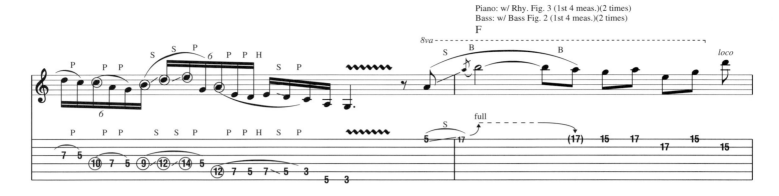

Piano: w/ Rhy. Fig. 3 (1st 4 meas.)(2 times)
Bass: w/ Bass Fig. 2 (1st 4 meas.)(2 times)

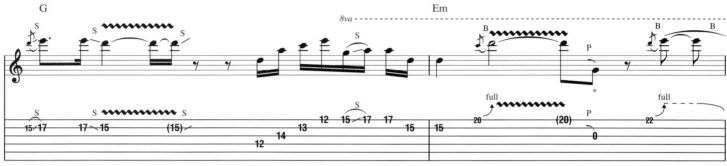

* Left hand sounds string as bend is released.

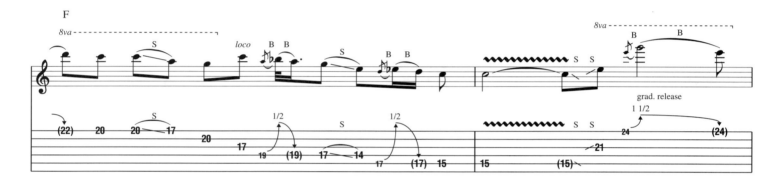

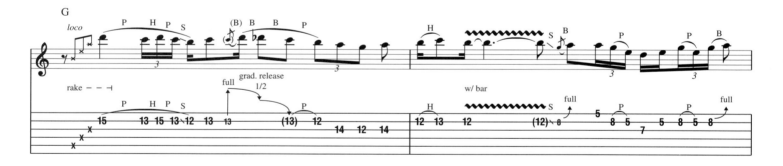

Piano: w/ Rhy. Fig. 3
Bass: w/ Bass Fig. 2

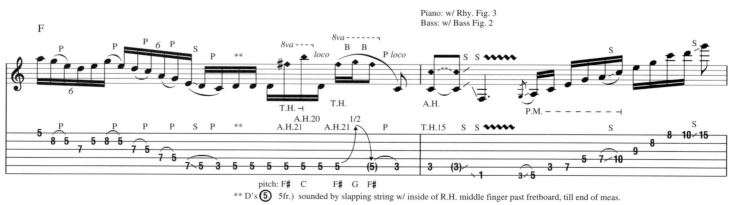

pitch: F#   C   F# G F#
** D's ⑤ 5fr.) sounded by slapping string w/ inside of R.H. middle finger past fretboard, till end of meas.

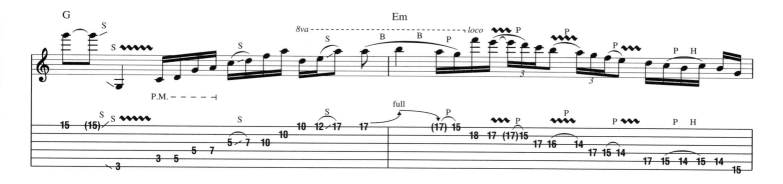

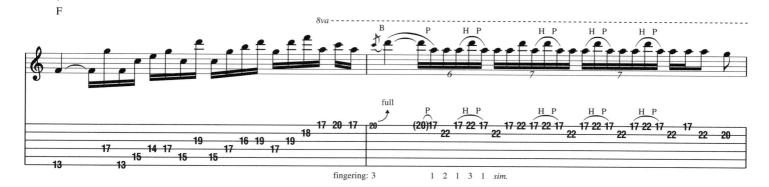

fingering: 3   1 2 1 3 1 *sim.*

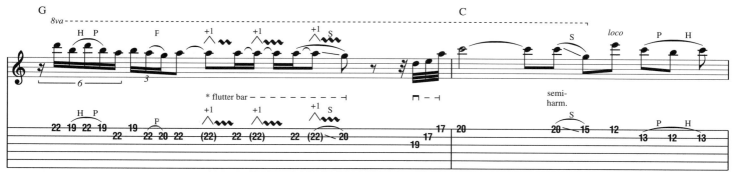

* Point vibrato bar at lower strap button, quickly depress, and let spring back.

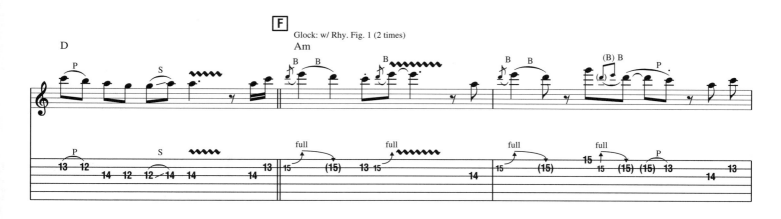

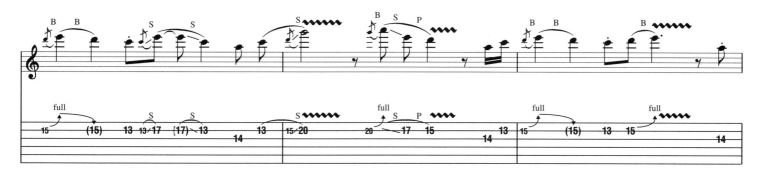

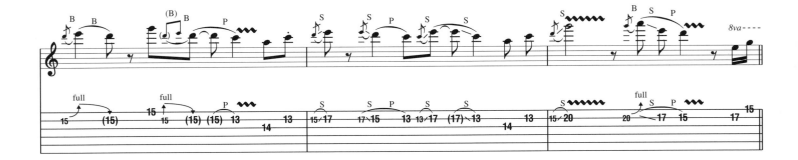

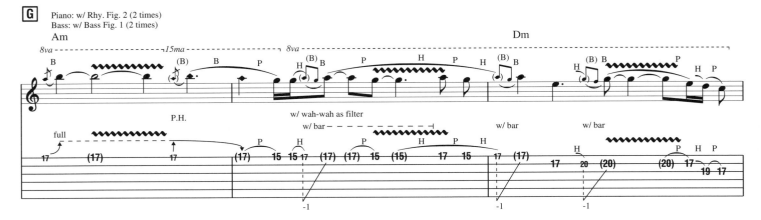

G Piano: w/ Rhy. Fig. 2 (2 times)
Bass: w/ Bass Fig. 1 (2 times)

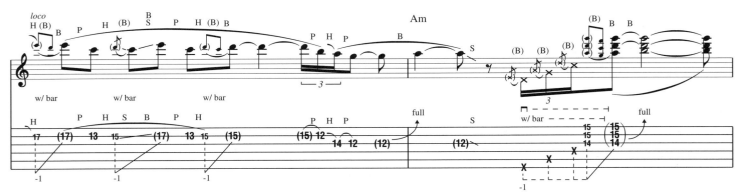

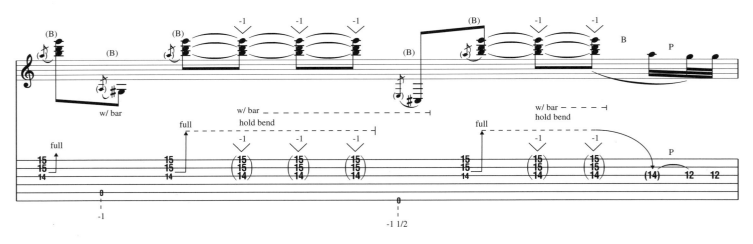

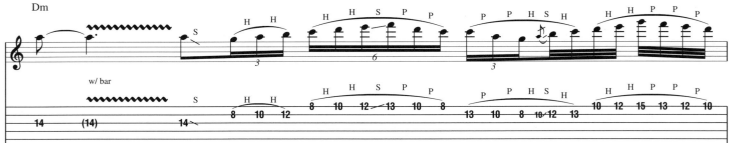

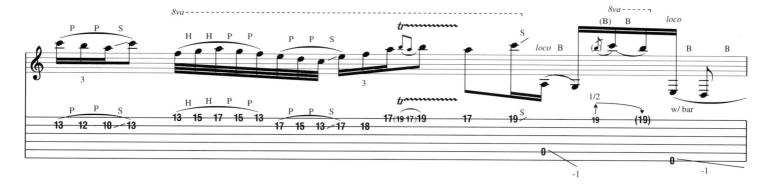

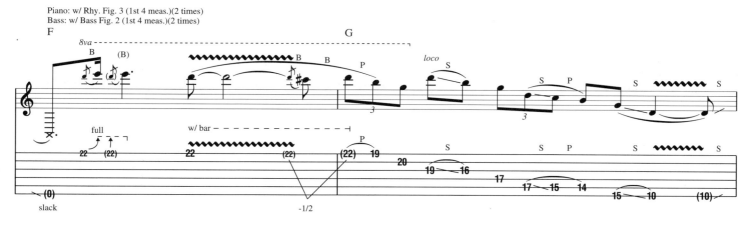

Piano: w/ Rhy. Fig. 3 (1st 4 meas.)(2 times)
Bass: w/ Bass Fig. 2 (1st 4 meas.)(2 times)

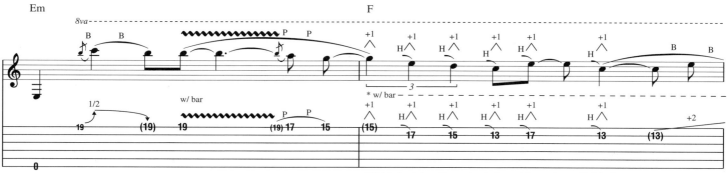

* Point vibrato bar at lower strap button and depress in specified rhythm.

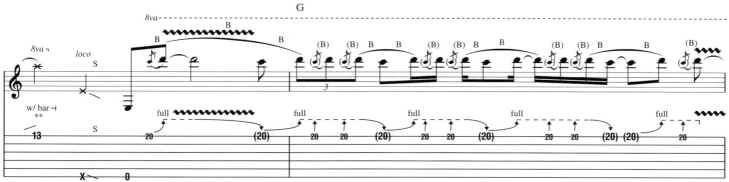

** Continue pushing down on bar until string "frets out" at approx. 20th fret.

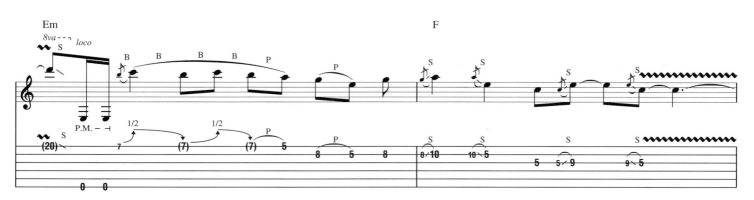

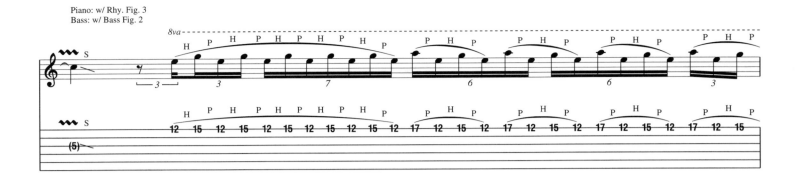

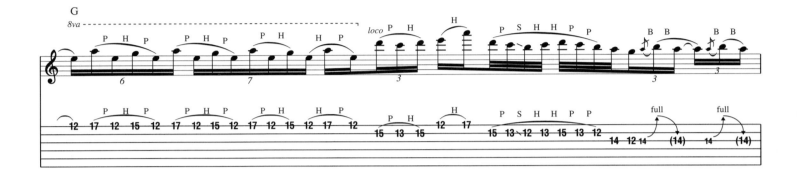

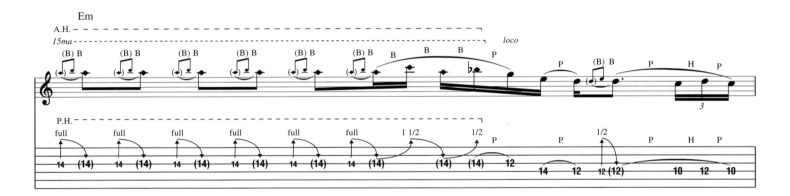

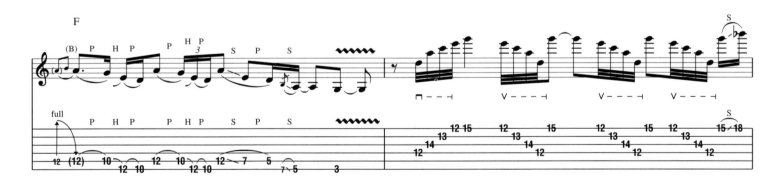

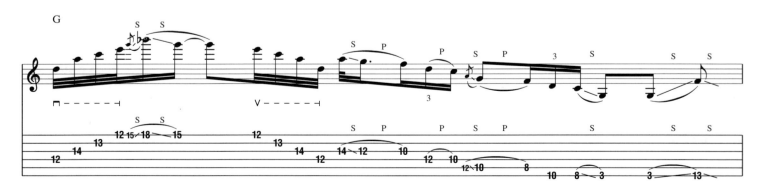

110

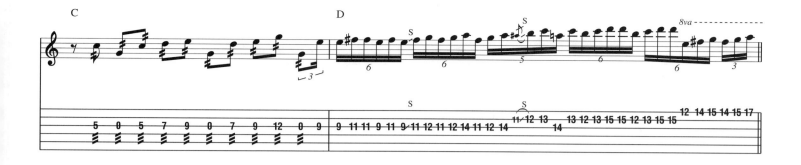

H Piano: w/ Rhy. Fig. 2 (4 times)
Bass: w/ Bass Fig. 1 (4 times)

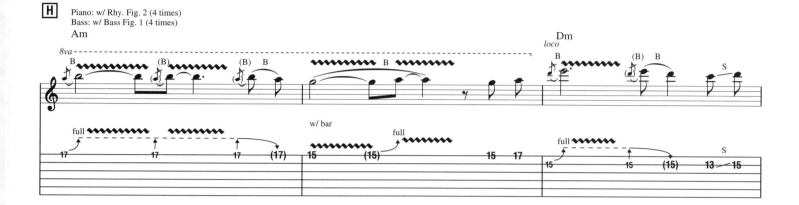

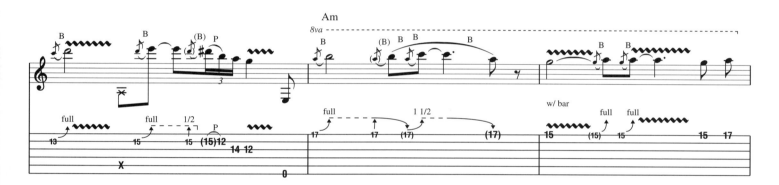

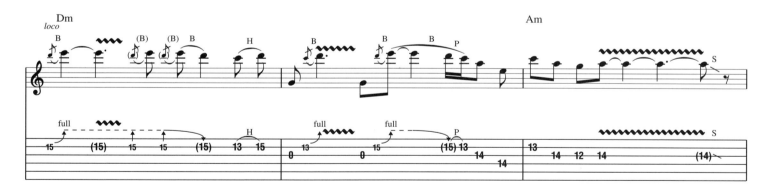

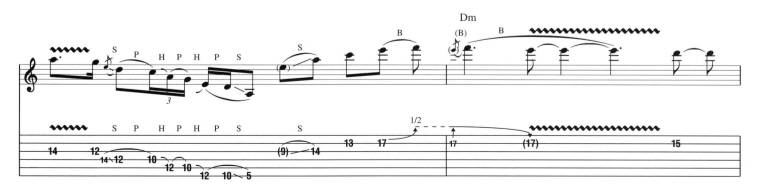

The Silent Within

Words and Music by Steve Vai

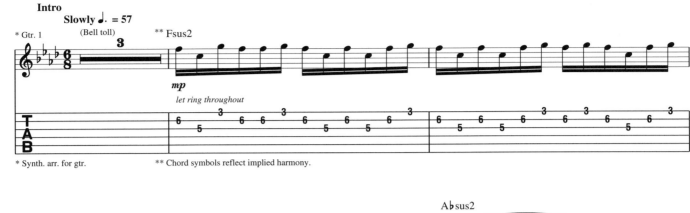

* Synth. arr. for gtr. ** Chord symbols reflect implied harmony.

*** Elec. sitar arr. for gtr.

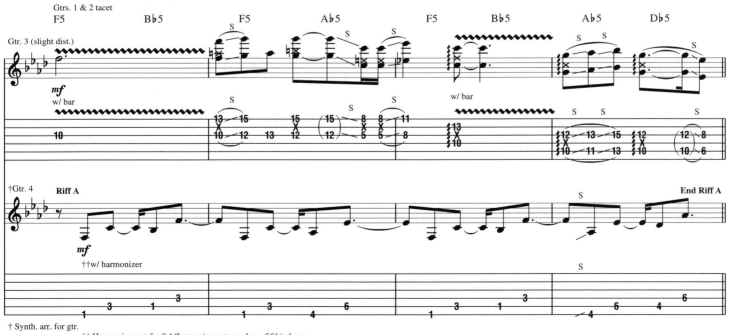

† Synth. arr. for gtr.

†† Harmonizer set for 9 1/2 steps (an octave plus a fifth) above.

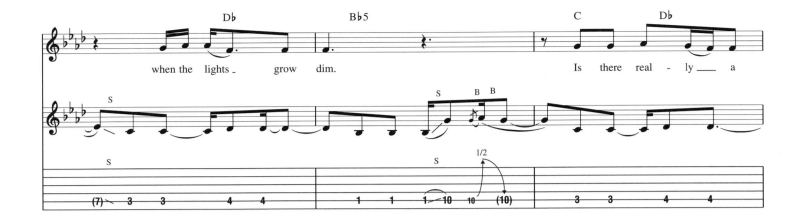

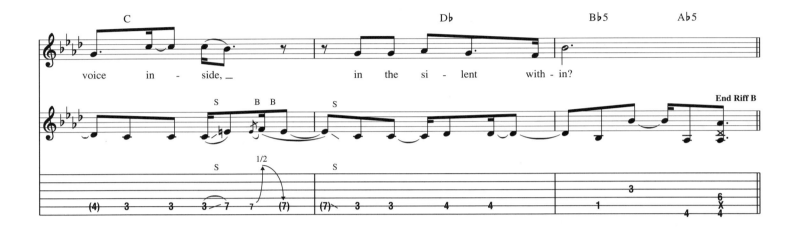

Verse

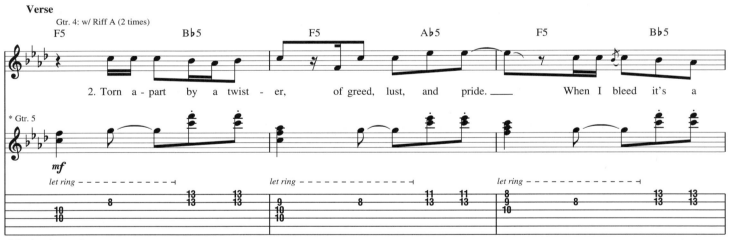

* Synth. strings arr. for gtr.

116

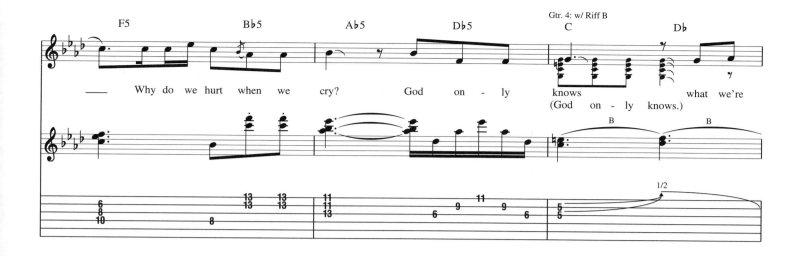

Why do we hurt when we cry? God on‑ly knows what we're
(God on‑ly knows.)

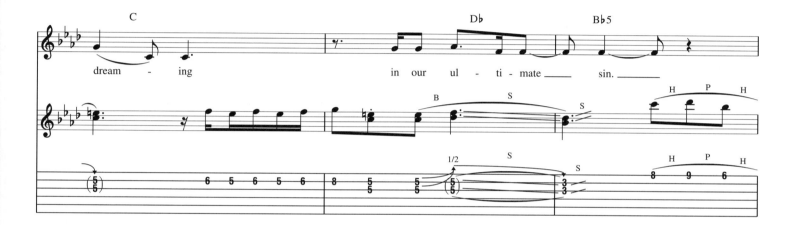

dream‑ing in our ul‑ti‑mate ___ sin. ___

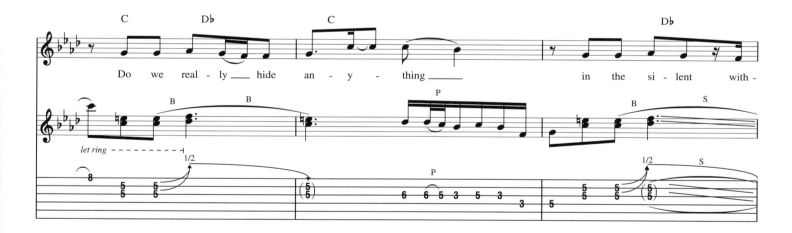

Do we real‑ly ___ hide an‑y‑thing ___ in the si‑lent with‑

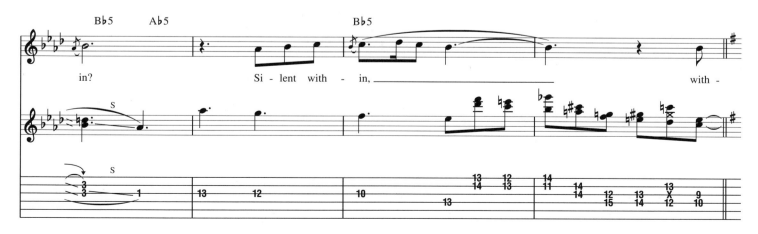

in? Si‑lent with‑in, ___ with‑

Bridge

in.
    (Oo,   hide in your dark - ness.   And I'm dream-ing to - day.   On - ly for a mo-ment would you

* Key signature denotes C Lydian.

hear? _____   Oo,   slow me down.   Run a - way.) _____   God on - ly
    (Run a, run a - way.) _____

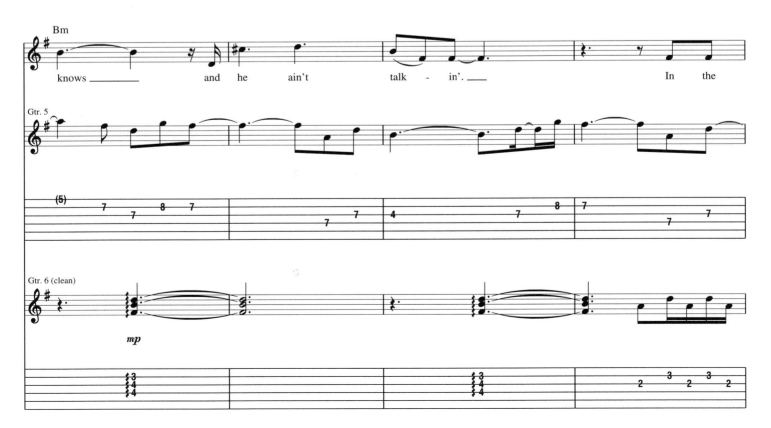

knows _____   and he ain't   talk - in'. _____   In the

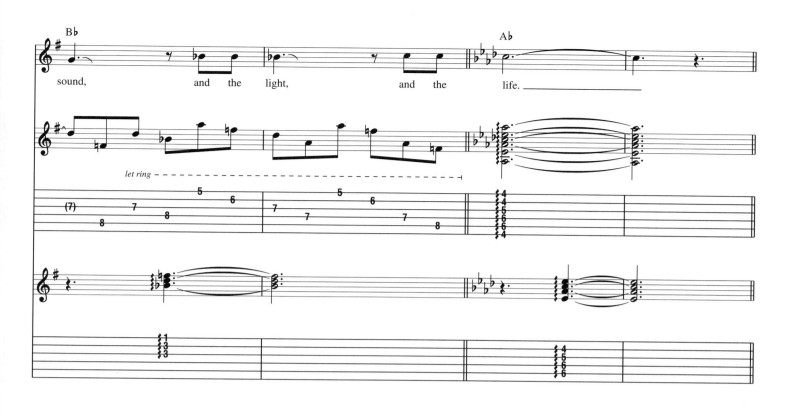

sound,　　　　and the light,　　　　and the life. _____

Verse

Gtr. 4: w/ Riff A (2 times)
Gtrs. 5 & 6 tacet

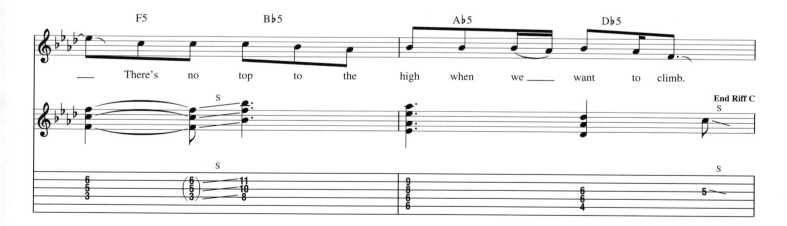

3. There's　no　end　to the bot-tom _____　when　we　start　to　fall. _____

Gtr. 3 **Riff C**

mp
w/ dist.

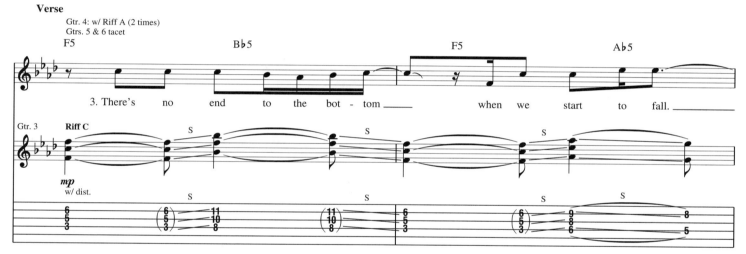

_____　There's　no　top　to the　high　when　we _____　want　to　climb.

End Riff C

Gtr. 3: w/ Riff C

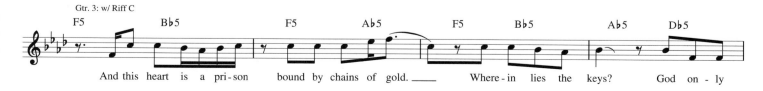

And this heart is a pri-son　bound by chains of gold. _____　Where-in lies the keys?　God on-ly

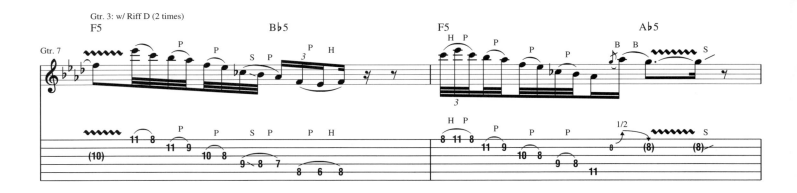

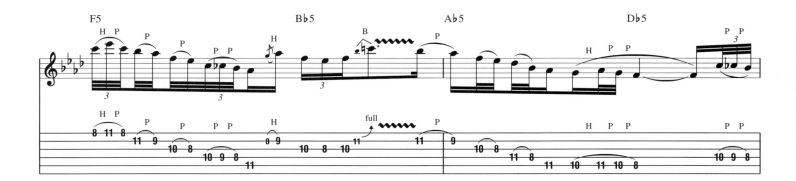

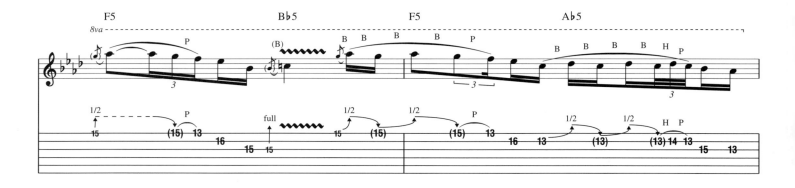

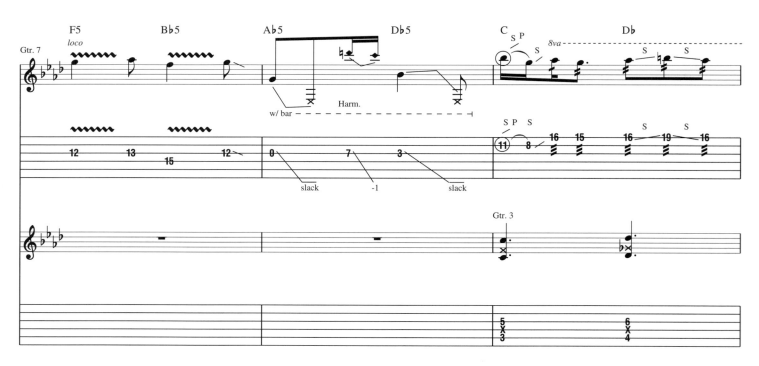

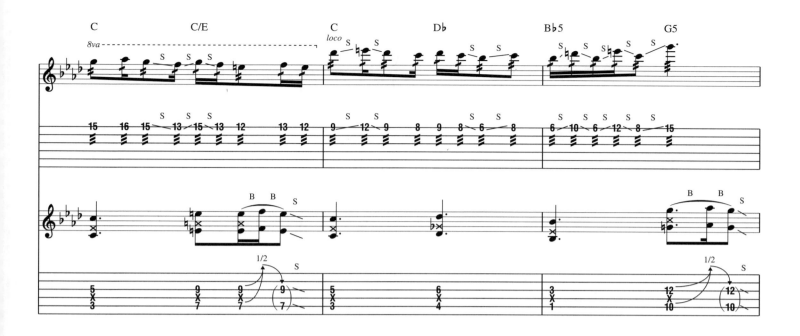

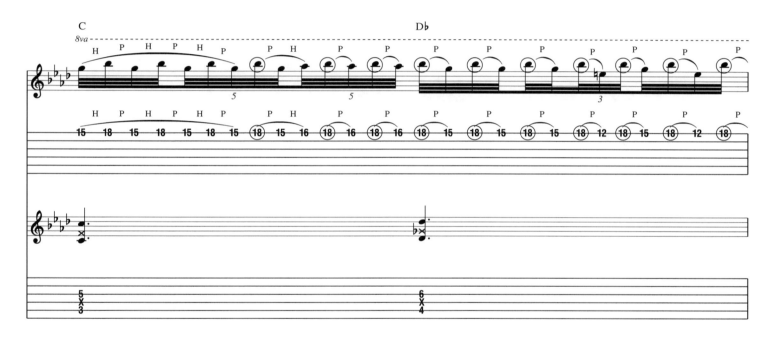

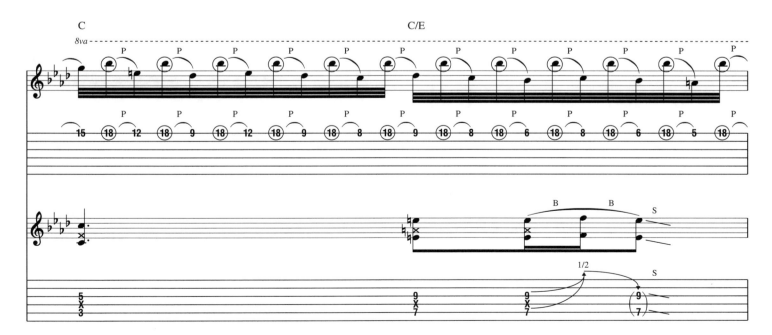

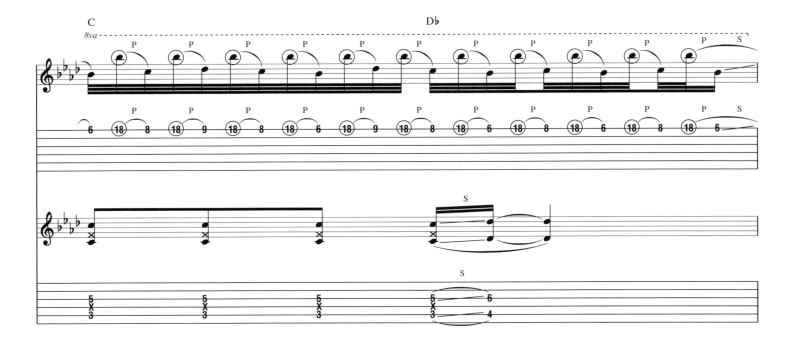

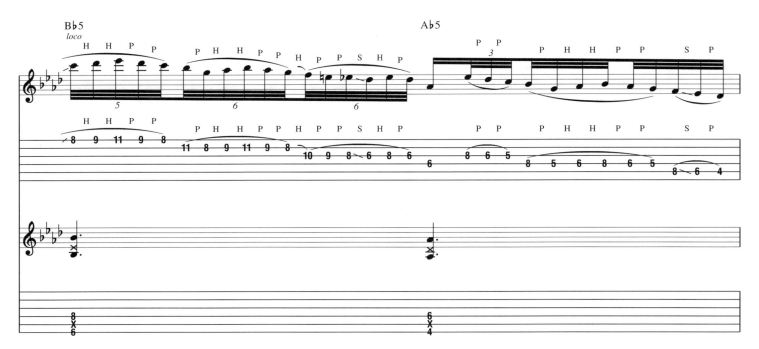

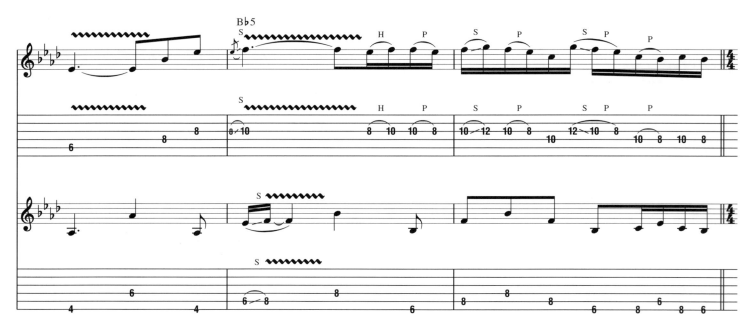

I'll Be Around

Words and Music by Steve Vai

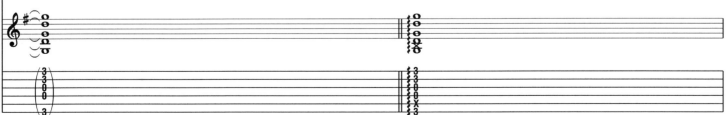

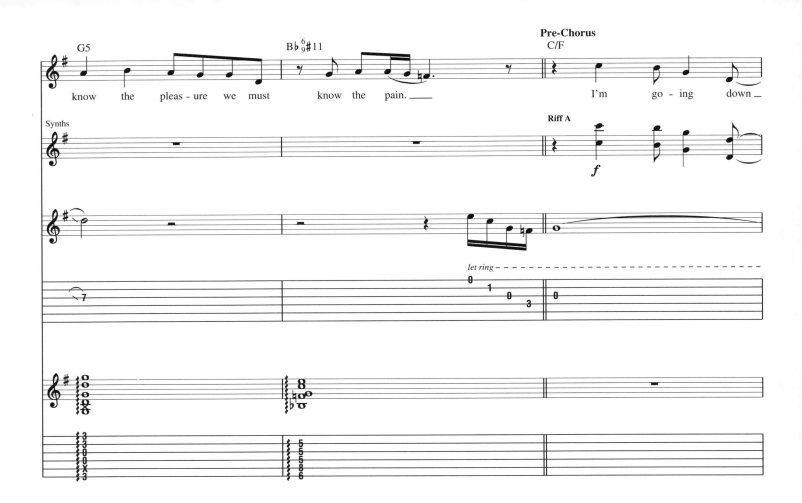

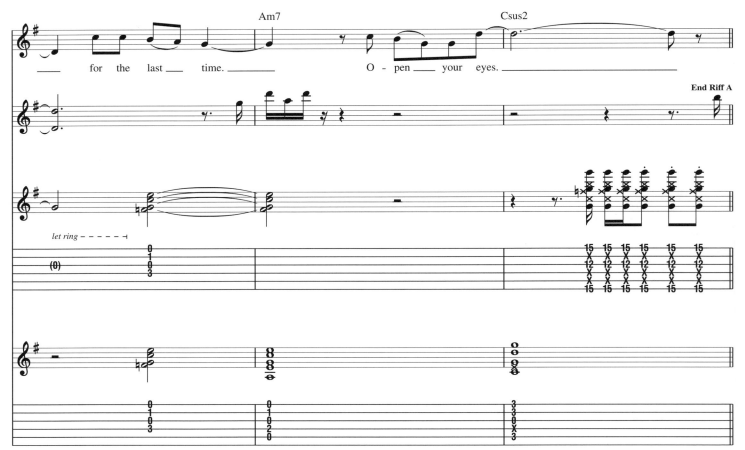

3rd time, Gtr. 3: w/ Fill 2

Who's gon-na hear _ you when you're call - in'? And who's gon-na catch _ you when you're fall - in'? And

Synths

Rhy. Fig. 1

*Gtrs. 1 & 2

*Composite arrangement

Who's gon-na { trust _ you? / laugh _ with you? / trust _ you? } Well, I'll be _ a - round for _ a while. _____ And

End Rhy. Fig. 1

T T *sim.*

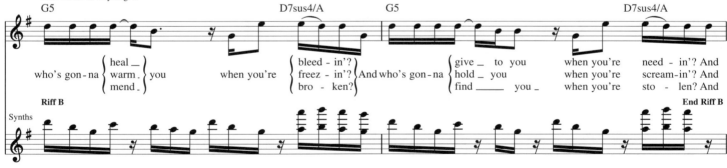

Gtrs. 1 & 2: w/ Rhy. Fig. 1

who's gon-na { heal _ / warm _ } you when you're { bleed - in'? / freez - in'? / bro - ken? } And who's gon-na { give _ to you / hold _ you / find ____ you _ } when you're { need - in'? And / scream-in'? And / sto - len? And }

Riff B **End Riff B**

Synths

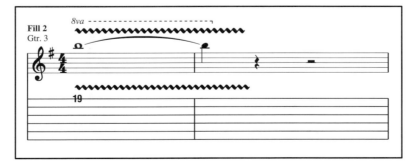

Fill 2
Gtr. 3

8va -

19

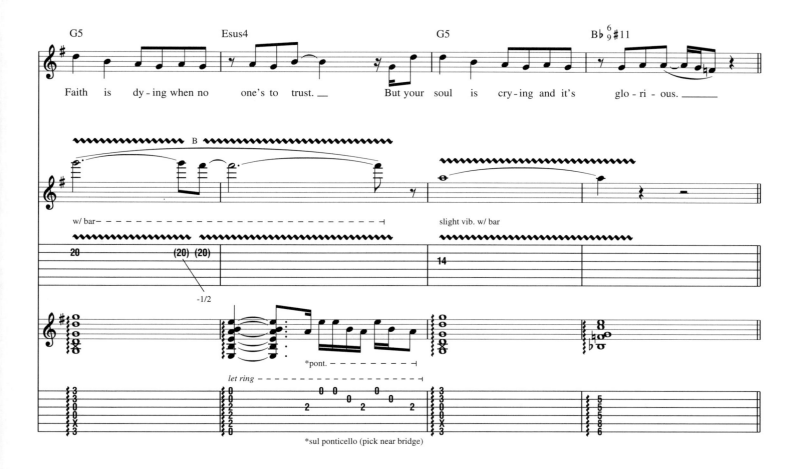

D.S. al Coda 1

Pre-Chorus

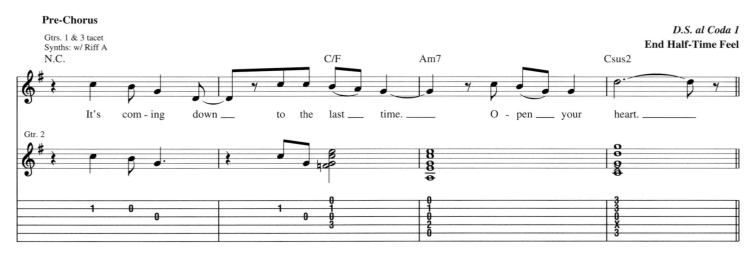

⊕ Coda 1

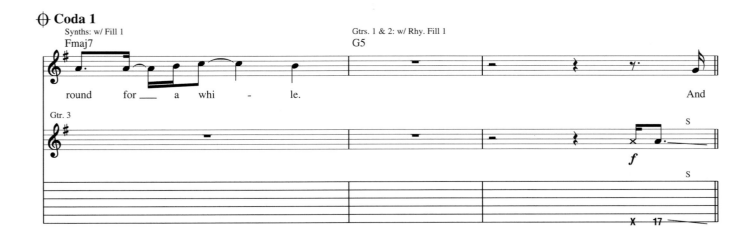

Bridge

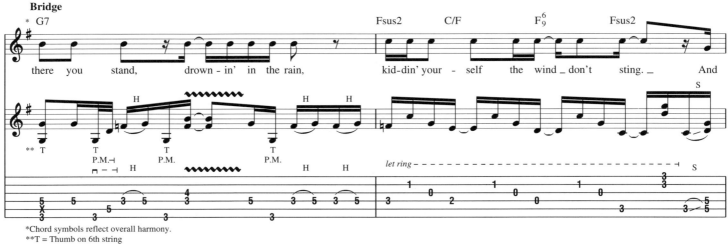

*Chord symbols reflect overall harmony.
**T = Thumb on 6th string

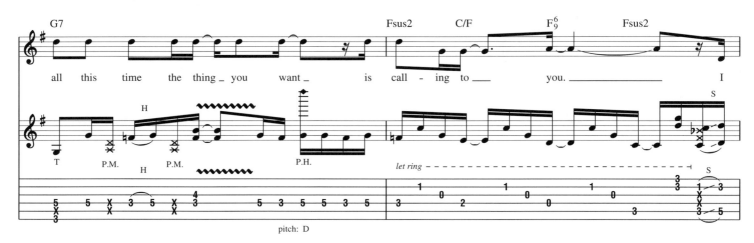

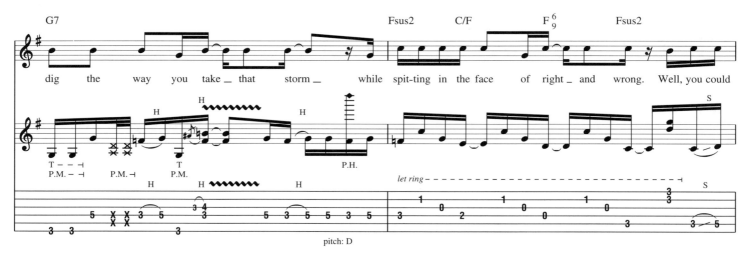

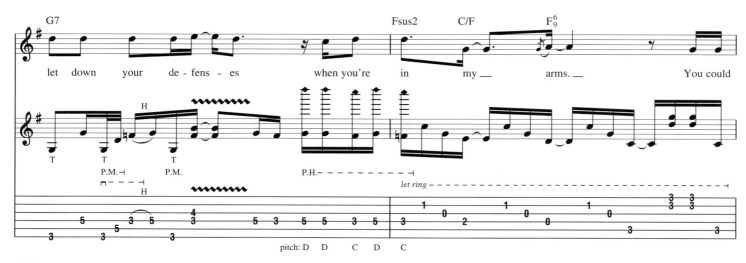

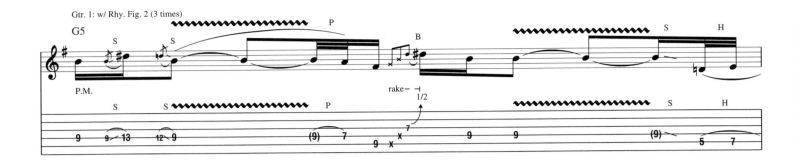

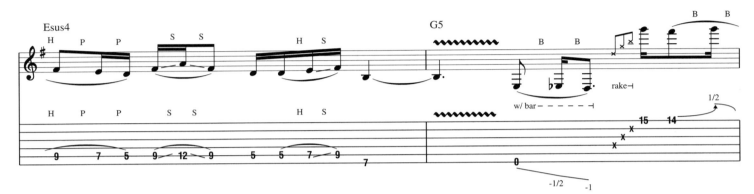

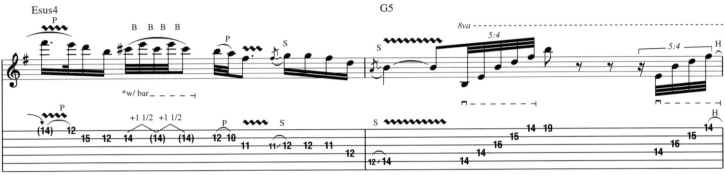

*Point vibrato bar at lower strap button, and depress in specified rhythm.

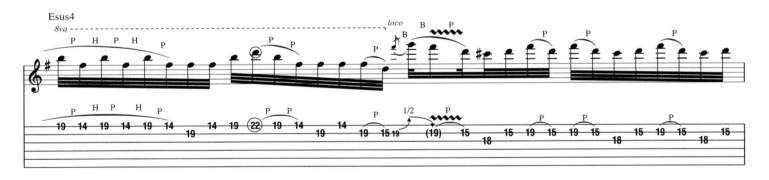

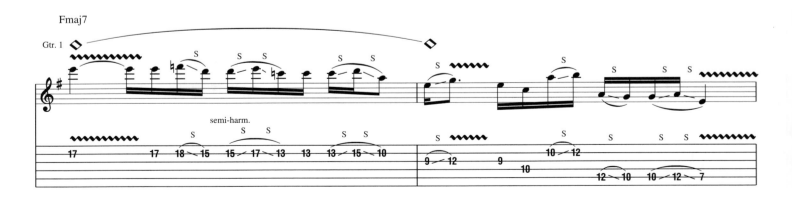

Coda 2

round   for ___ a   whi - le.   And   who's gon - na   shield ___   you   when it's   rain - in'? And

who's gon - na   kneel ___ with you ___ when you're   pray - in'?   Who's gon - na   feel ___   for you? ___   Well, I   will; I'll   be a -

round   for ___ a   whi -   le.   Who's gon - na   help ___   you ___   when you're   try - in'? And

who's gon - na   hold ___   you ___   when you're   dy - in'?   Who's gon - na   beg ___   you ___   to   be ___   a - round   for ___ a   while? ___

Lucky Charms

By Steve Vai

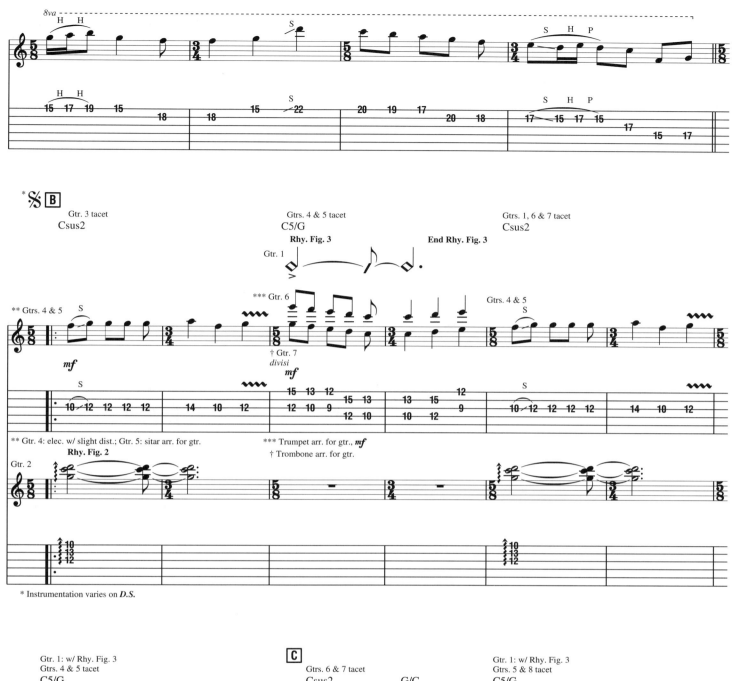

* Instrumentation varies on *D.S.*

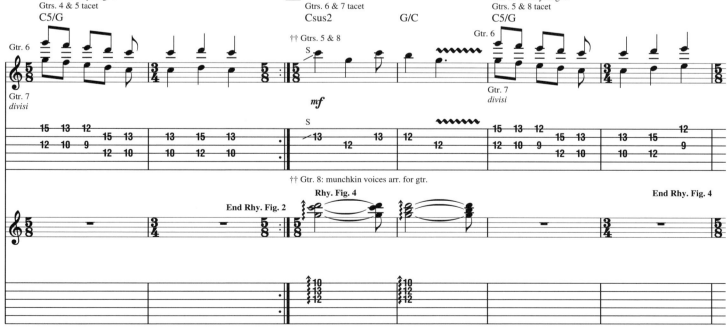

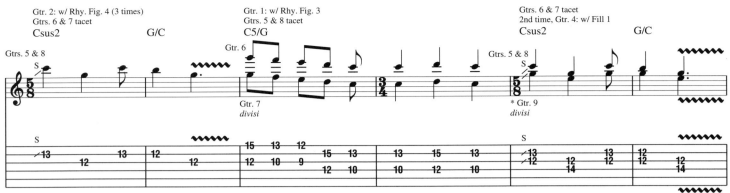

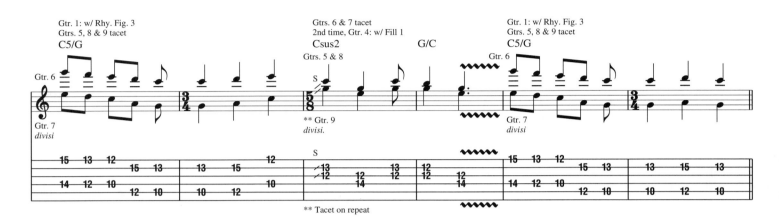

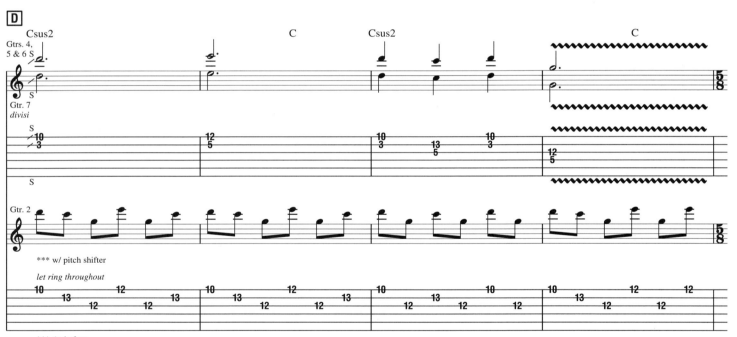

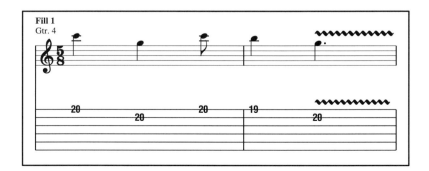

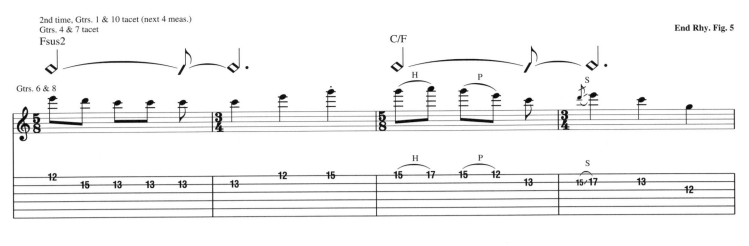

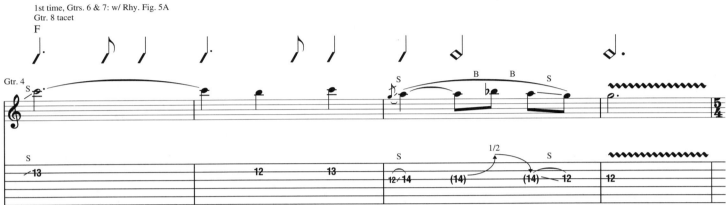

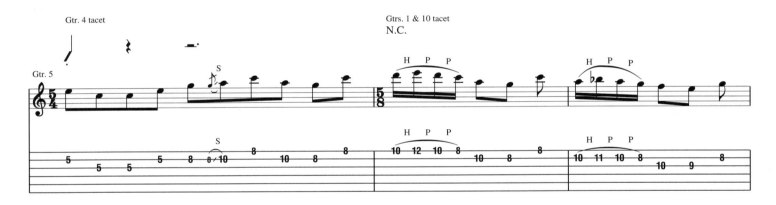

140

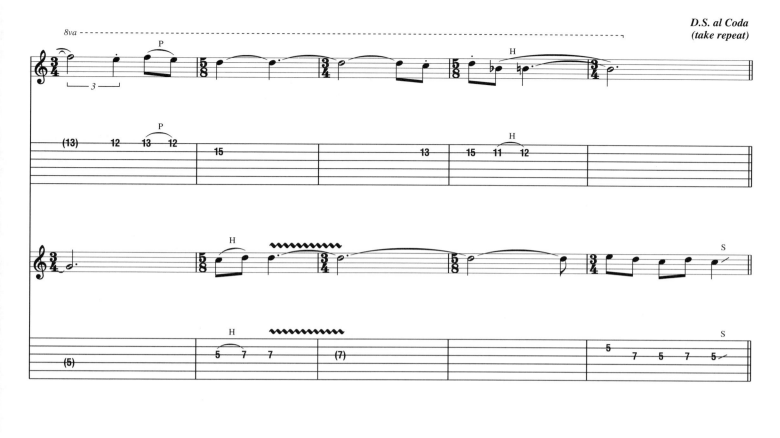

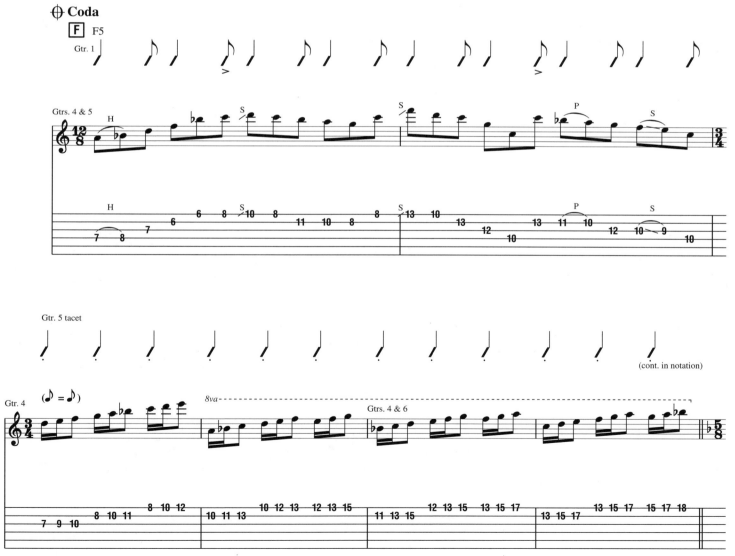

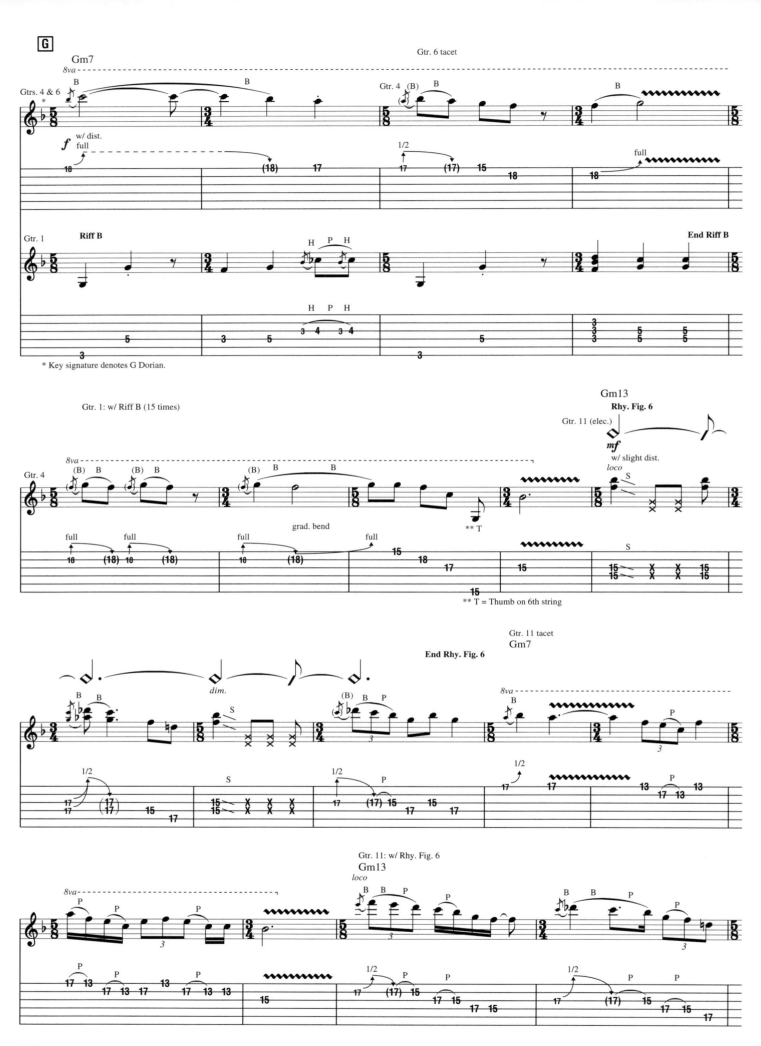

* Key signature denotes G Dorian.

** T = Thumb on 6th string

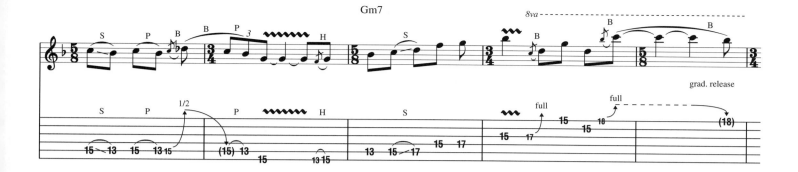

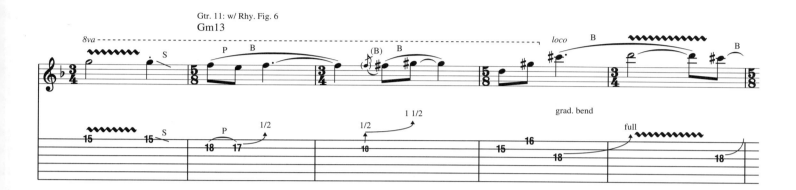

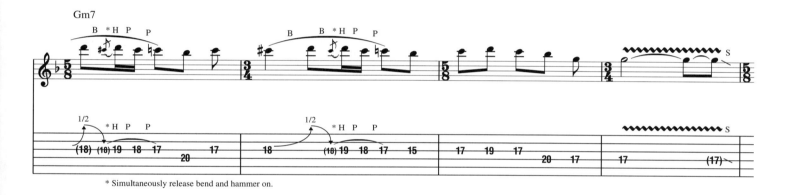

* Simultaneously release bend and hammer on.

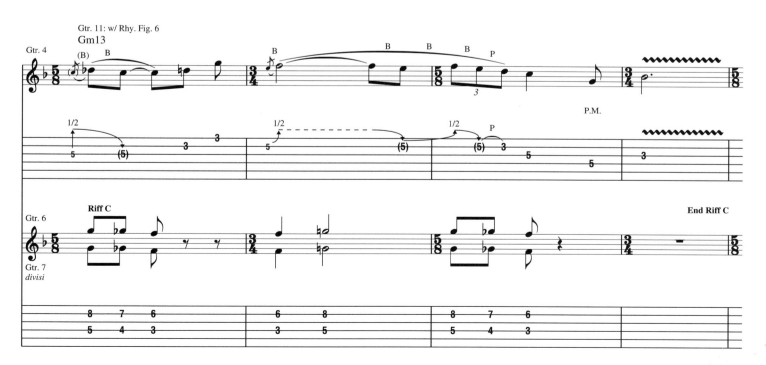

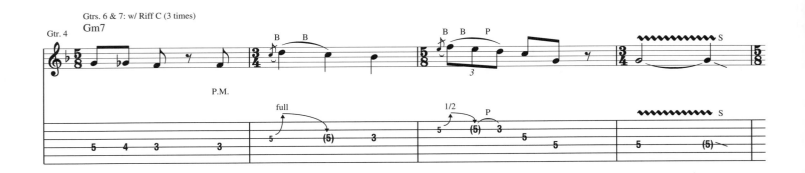

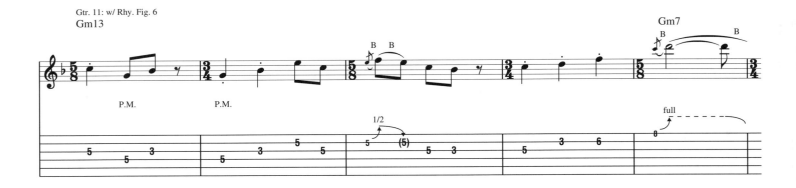

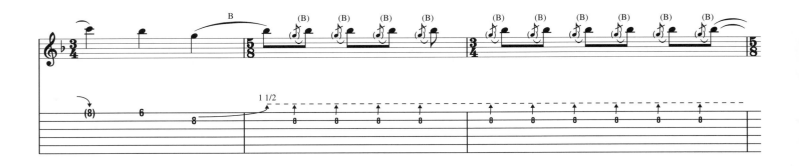

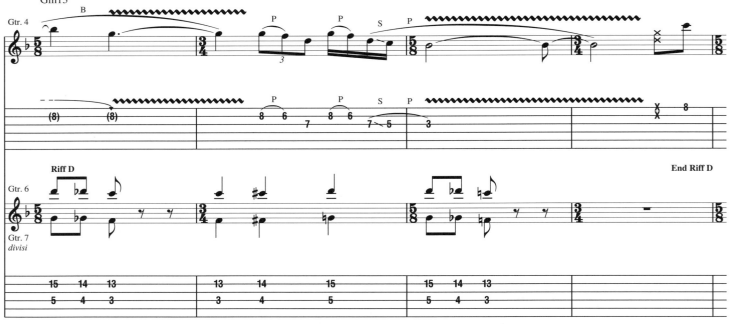

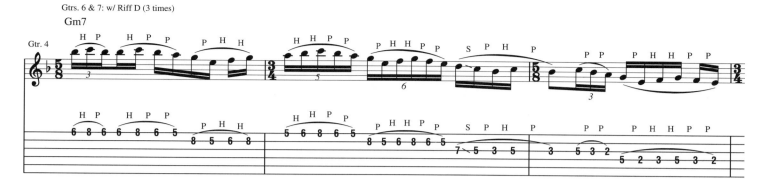

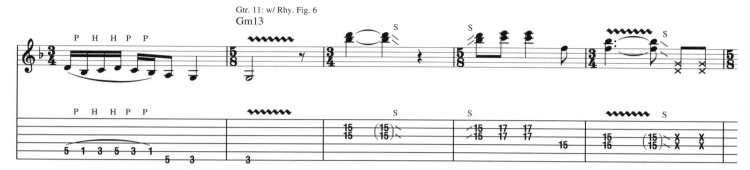

Gtr. 6: w/ Riff E (2 times)
Gtrs. 7 & 11 tacet

* Synth. flutes arr. for gtr., *mp*

** Bells/ pizzicato strings arr. for gtr.

*** Pizzicato strings arr. for gtr.

146

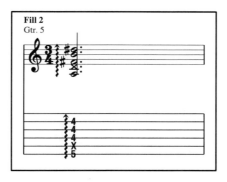

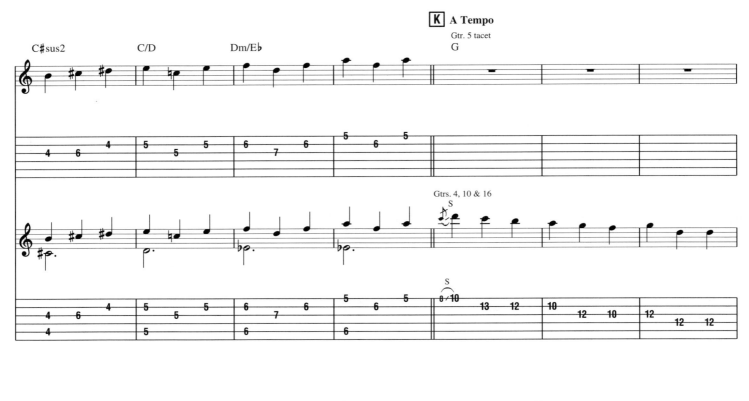

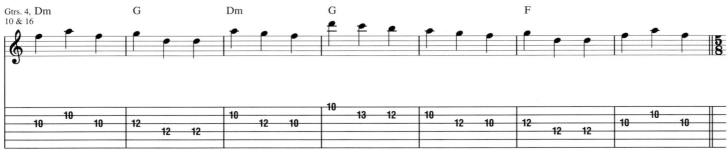

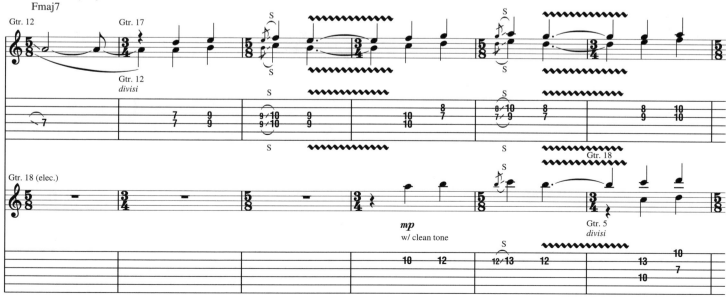

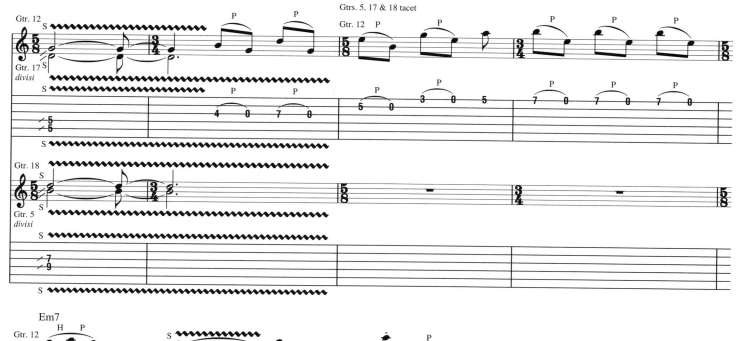

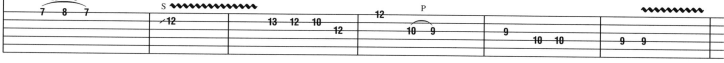

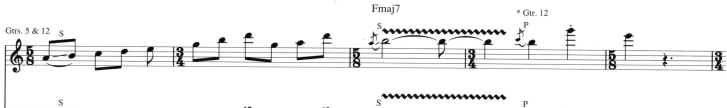

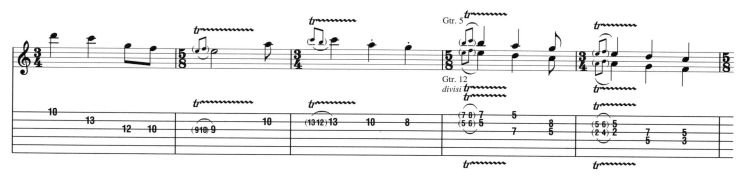

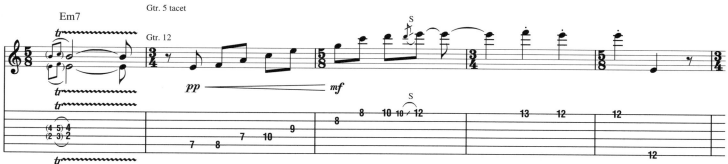

152

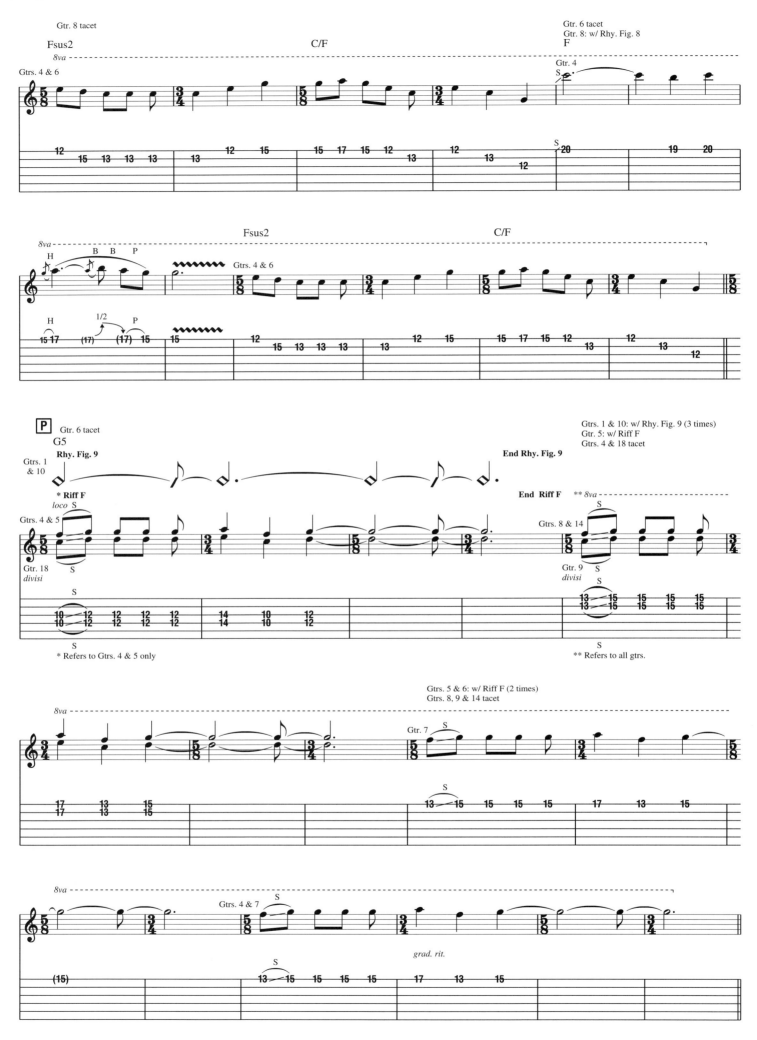

154

Fever Dream

By Steve Vai

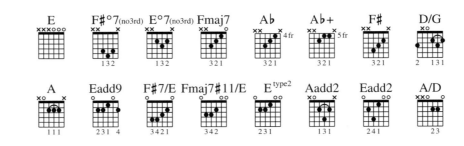

Gtr. 2: tuning:
(low to high) E–A–D–G#–B–E
Gtr. 3: Open A tuning, capo VII:
(low to high) E–A–E–A–C#–E

A Moderately ♩ = 116

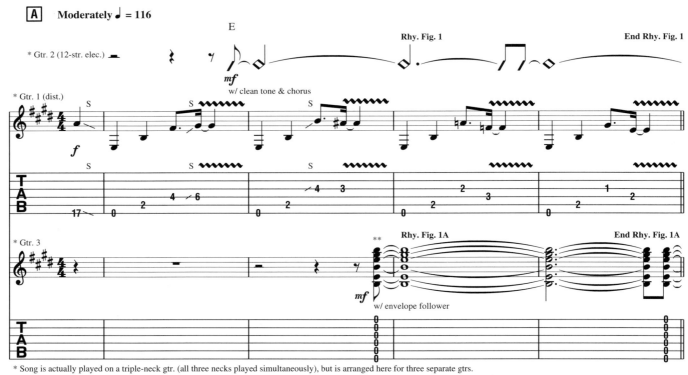

* Song is actually played on a triple-neck gtr. (all three necks played simultaneously), but is arranged here for three separate gtrs.

** Music sounds as written. Capoed fret is "0" in TAB.

B **Double-Time Feel**

Gtrs. 2 & 3: w/ Rhy. Figs. 1 & 1A (4 times)

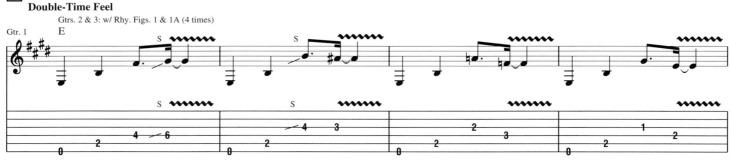

Double-Time Feel

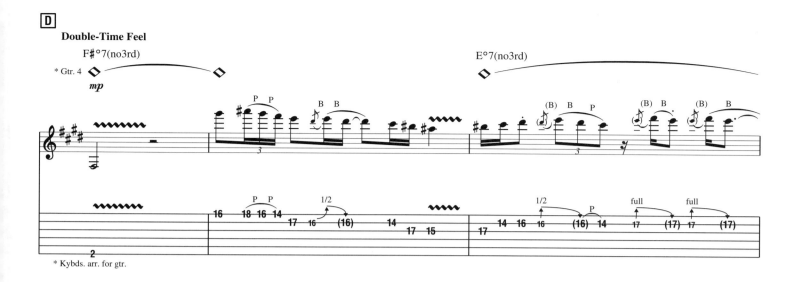

* Kybds. arr. for gtr.

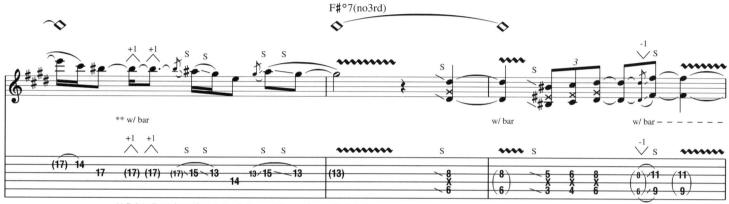

** Point vibrato bar at lower strap button and depress in specified rhythm.

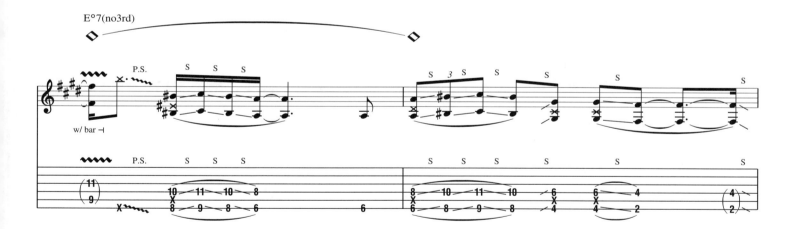

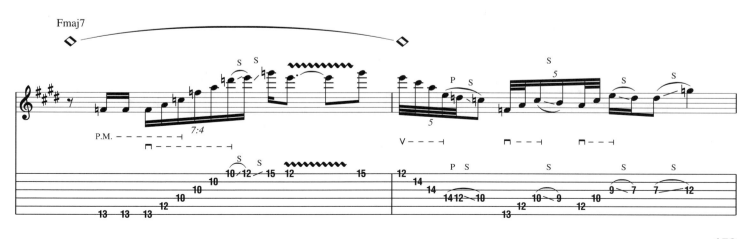

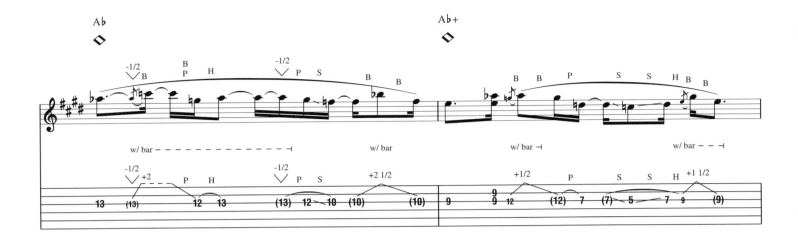

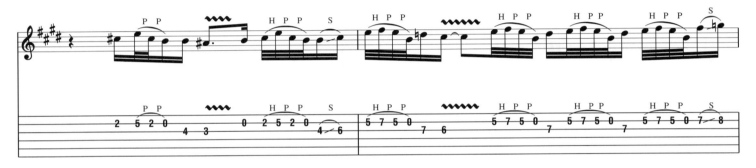

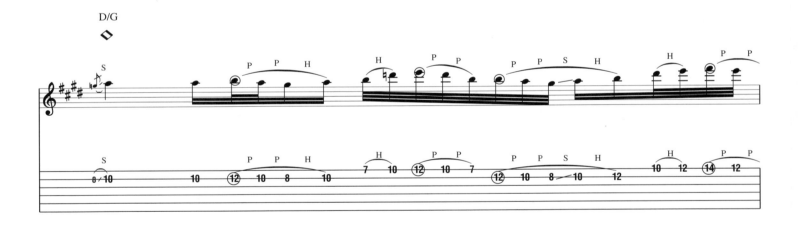

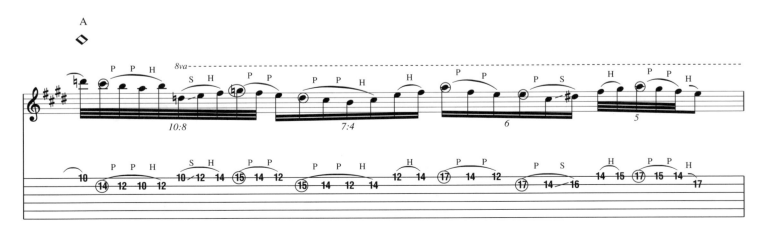

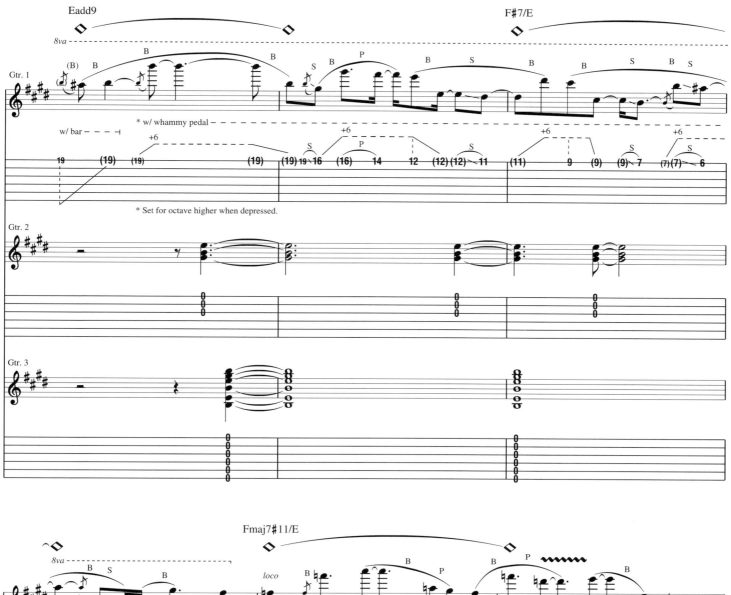

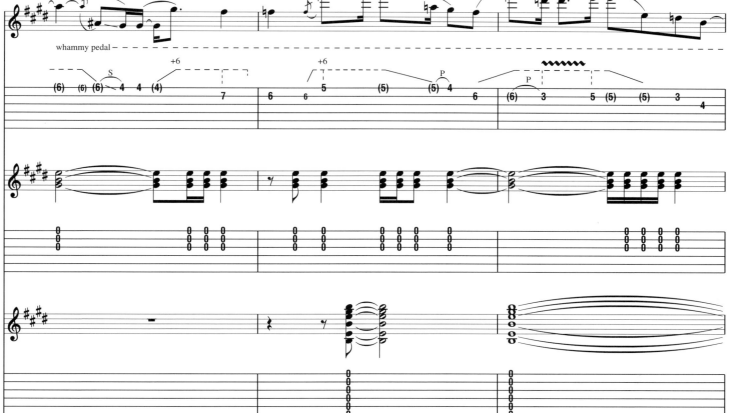

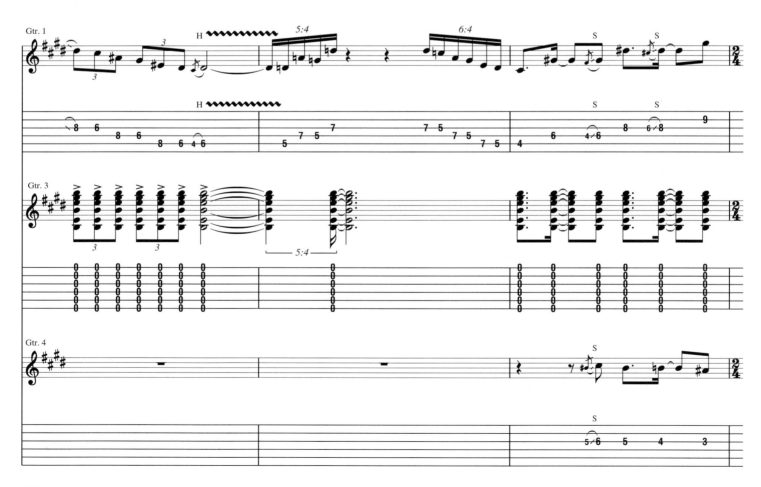

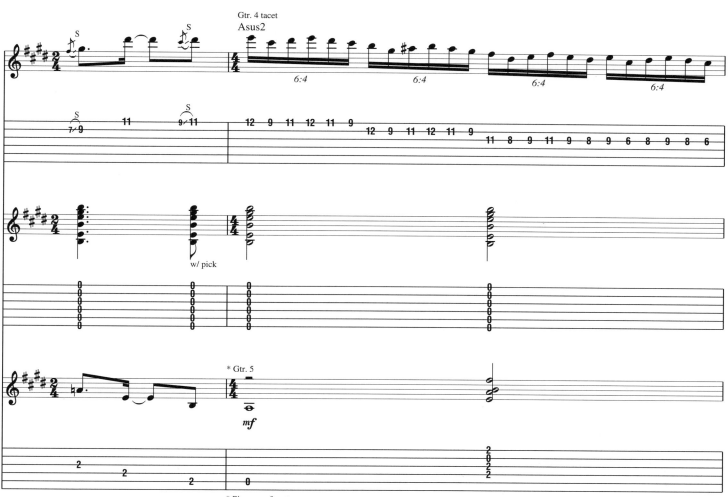

Gtr. 4 tacet

Asus2

w/ pick

* Gtr. 5

mf

* Piano arr. for gtr.

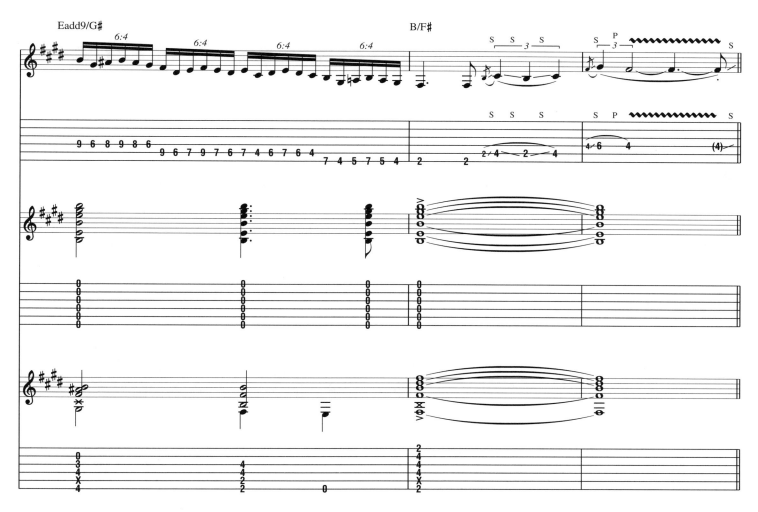

Eadd9/G#

B/F#

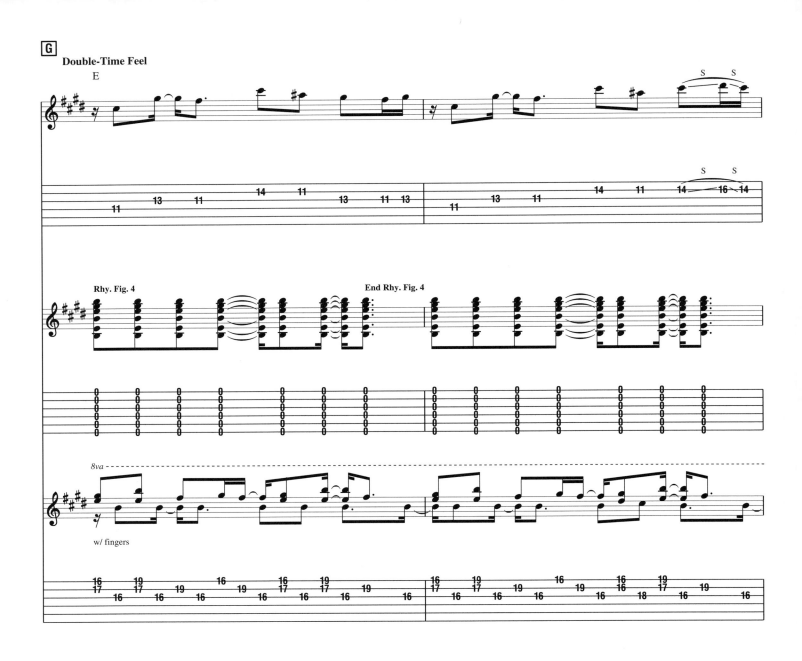

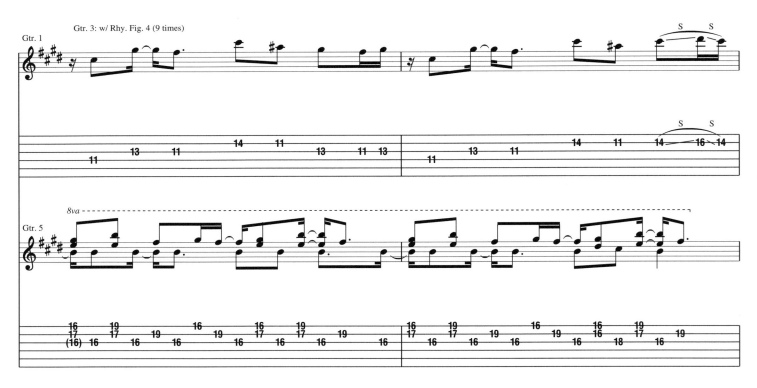

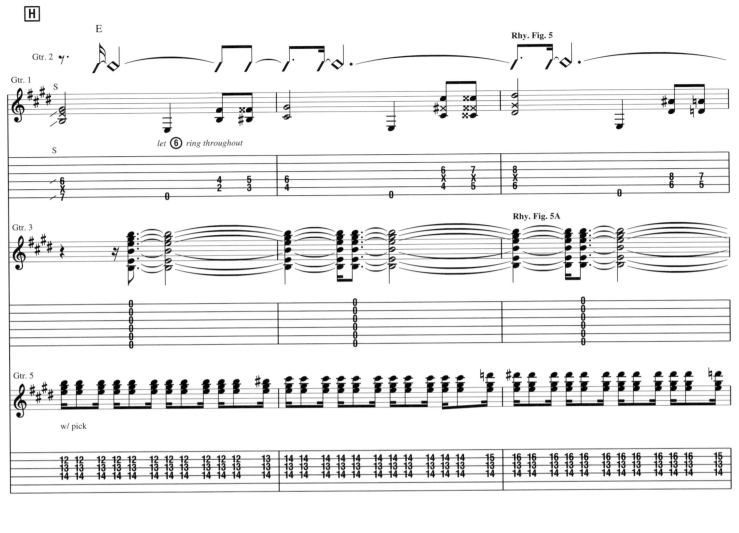

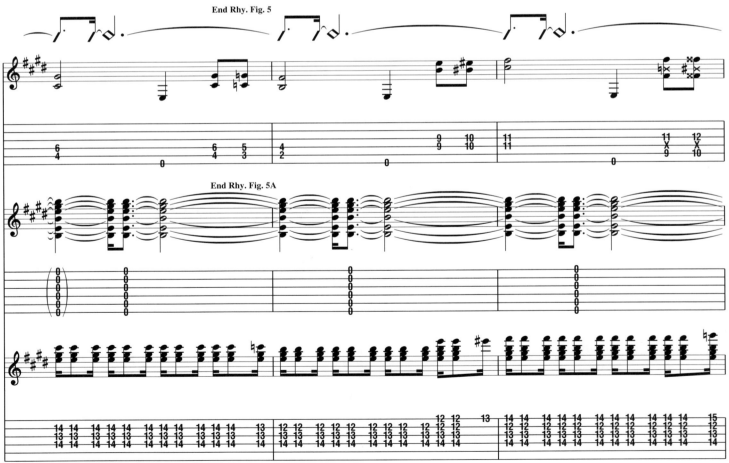

168

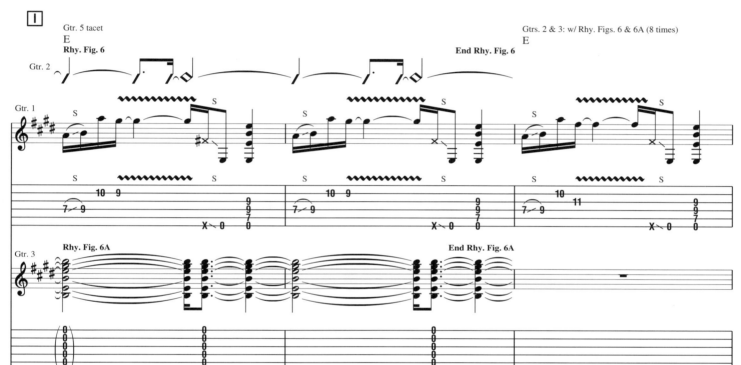

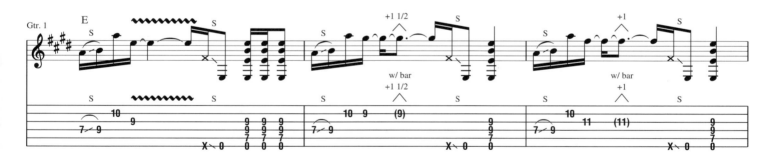

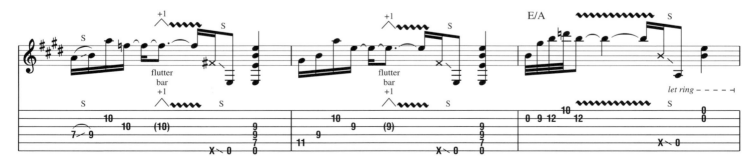

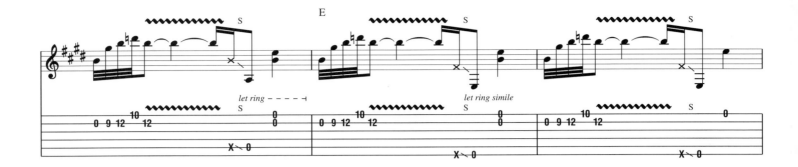

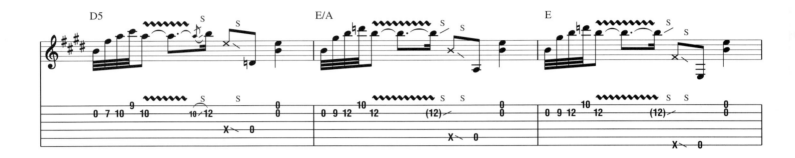

E

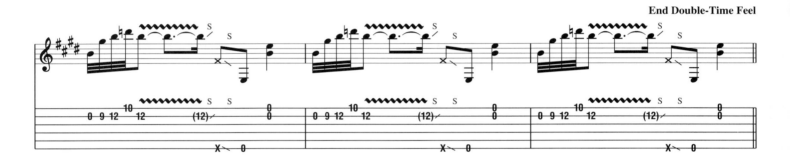

D5   E/A   E

End Double-Time Feel

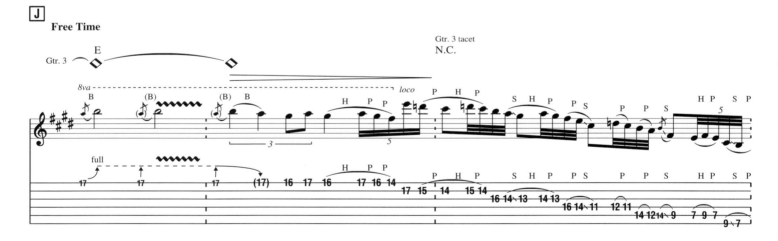

J **Free Time**

Gtr. 3 tacet
N.C.

Gtr. 3 E

K **A Tempo**
N.C.

Double-Time Feel

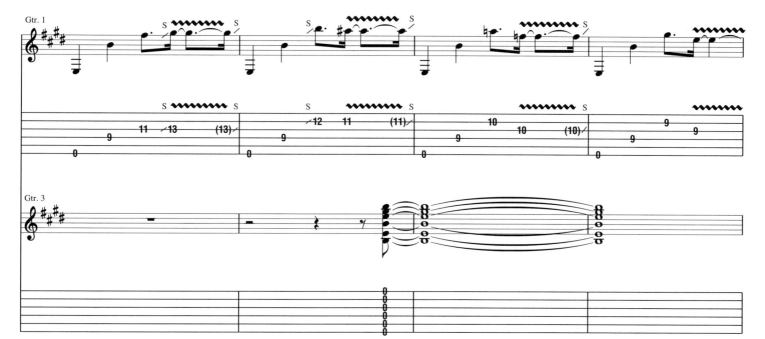

Gtr. 3: w/ Rhy. Fig. 2 (1st 11 meas., simile)

172

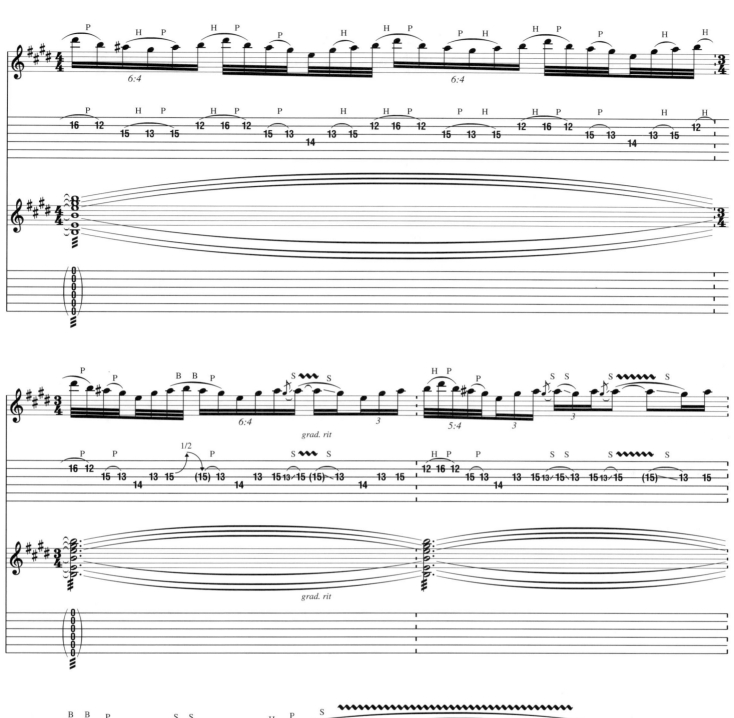
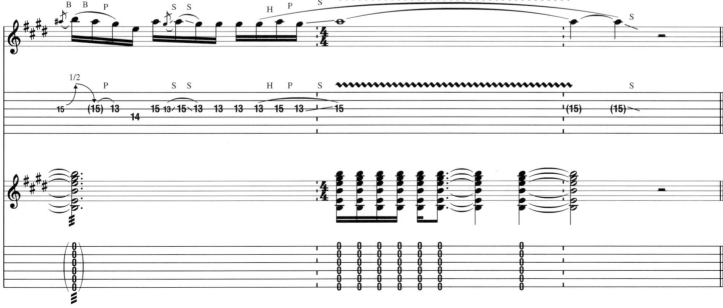

Here I Am

Words and Music by Steve Vai

Gtr. 3: w/ Rhy. Fill 4

A   D5   Em7   Gsus2   N.C.

I would treas-ure ev-'ry u - ni-verse that I ___ found. ___

Gtr. 3: w/ Rhy. Fig. 3

Em7   Gsus2   A   D5   Em7   Gsus2

Like a work of art, ___ it's beau-ty is bound - less and pro - found. ___

* Gtr. 4
to left of
slash in tab.

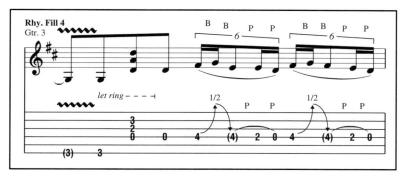

Rhy. Fill 4
Gtr. 3

let ring - - - ⌐

Pre-Chorus

D.S. al Coda

⊕ Coda

Guitar Solo

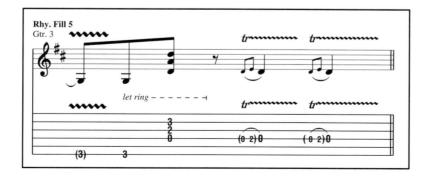

Pull bar up until string "frets out."

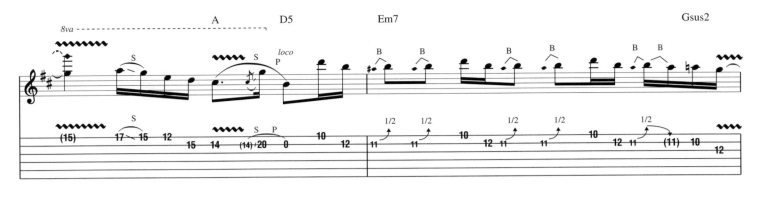

A D5 Em7 Gsus2

Gtr. 3: w/ Rhy. Fill 3 (simile)   Gtr. 3: w/ Rhy. Fig. 1 (1 3/4 times, simile)

N.C. Em7 Gsus2

*Tap w/ edge of pick on 1st str. only.

A D5

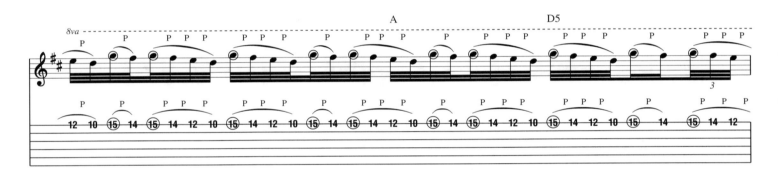

Em7 Gsus2

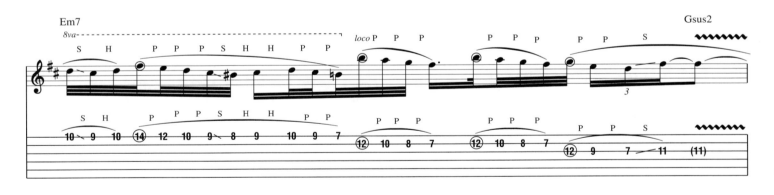

N.C. Em7 Gsus2

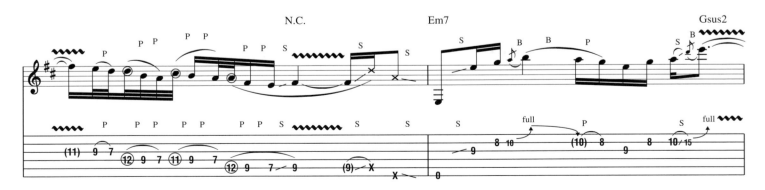

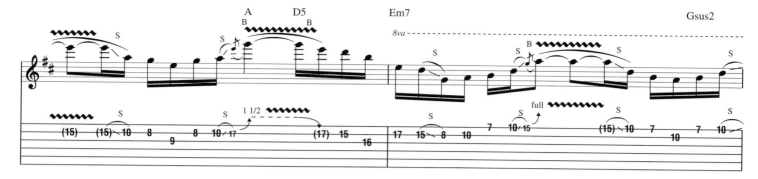

Gtr. 3: w/ Rhy. Fill 6

* Gtr. 3: w/ Rhy. Fig. 4 (1st 6 meas., simile)

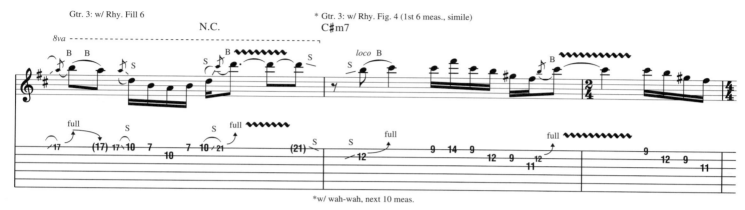

*w/ wah-wah, next 10 meas.

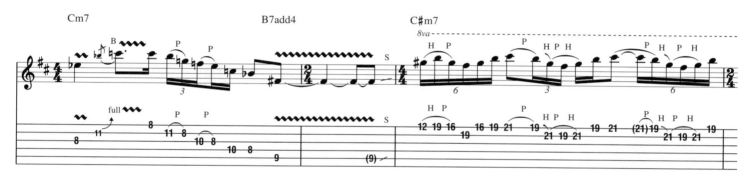

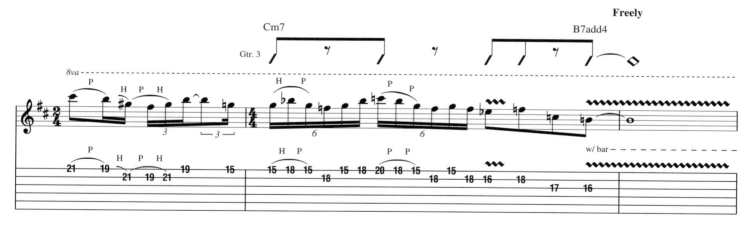

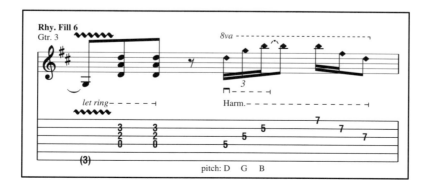

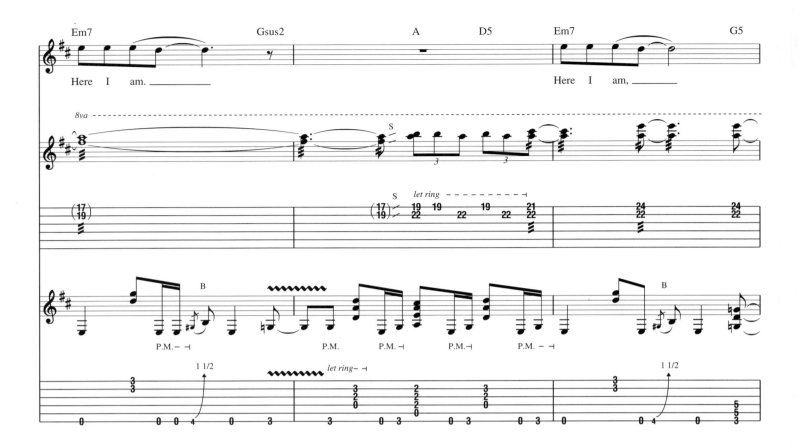

Here I am. _____

Here I am, _____

Free Time

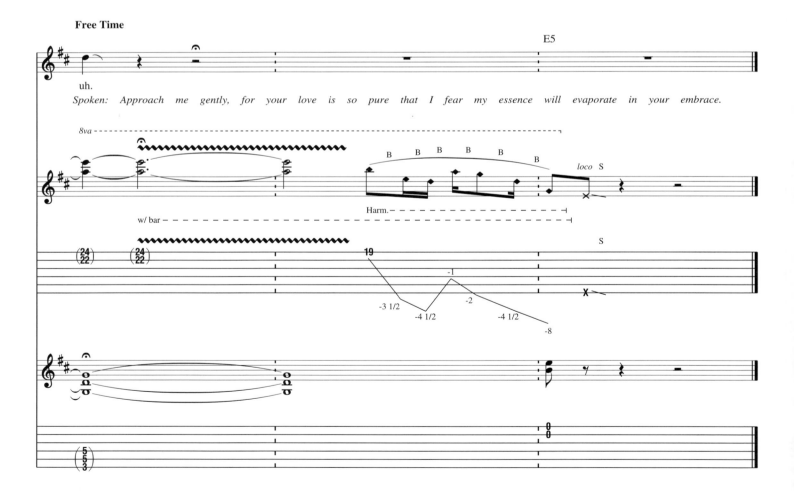

uh.

Spoken: Approach me gently, for your love is so pure that I fear my essence will evaporate in your embrace.

Asian Sky

Words and Music by Steve Vai, Tak Matsumoto and Kohshi Inaba

*Key signature denotes C# Mixolydian.

**Chord symbols reflect implied harmony.

†7-str. gtrs.; ⑦ tuned to low B

***w/ an Eventide 4000 voice filter setting producing a "Ya-ee" syllabic effect at quarter-note regeneration.

††Gtr. 1 doubled throughout

-ness   to   find   the ___ way ___   back   to   it's   lov-er's   arms. ___

(O-ver   and   o   -   ver.) ___

Gtr. 5 (dist.)

mf

1/2

End Rhy. Fig. 1

Gtr. 4

Pre-Chorus

Gtrs. 4 & 5 tacet

And through this   fate ___   they nev-er   un-der - stand _____

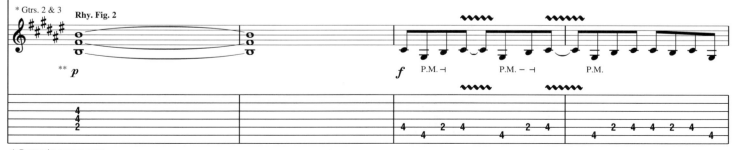

* Gtrs. 2 & 3   **Rhy. Fig. 2**

** *p*   *f*   P.M.   P.M.   P.M.

* Composite arrangement

** Played *f* when recalled

just how end - less ___ the sea. _____

___ It's hard to find ___ that

si - lent piece _ of mind. _ They die to _ be... ___ A -

End Rhy. Fig. 2

Chorus

Gtr. 1: w/ Riff A (2 times)
Gtrs. 2 & 3: w/ Riff A1

Gtr. 6: w/ Fill 2

live _____ in an A - sian sky. _____ A -

Fill 2
Gtr. 6 (clean)

8va -

mf

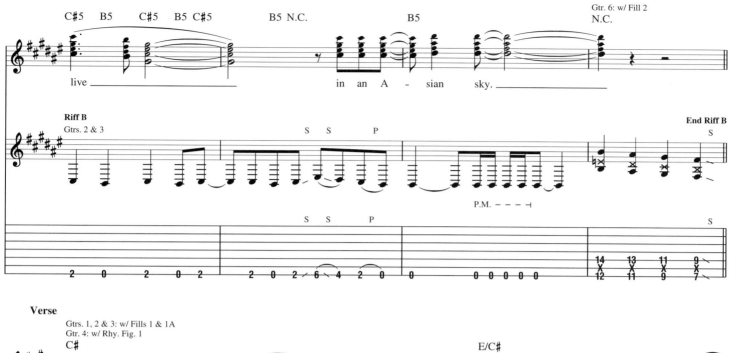

live _____   in an A - sian sky. _____

Verse

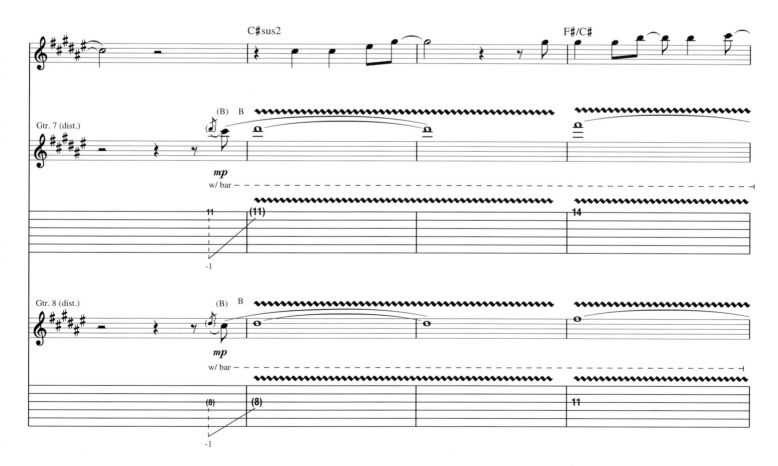

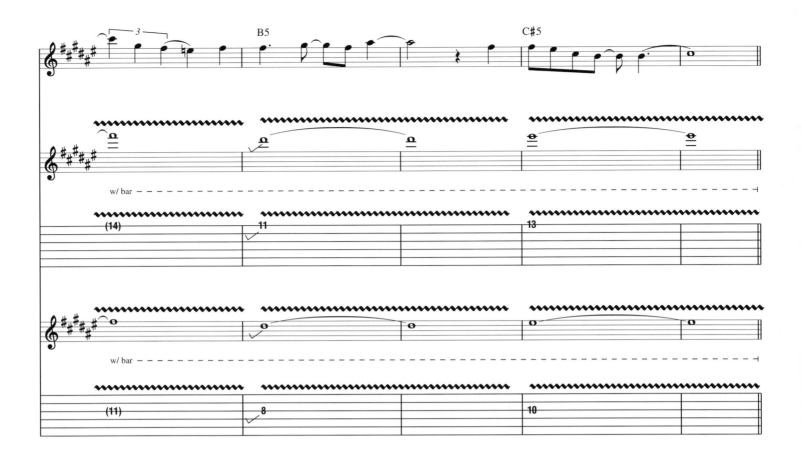

Pre-Chorus

Gtrs. 2 & 3: w/ Rhy. Fig. 2
Gtrs. 7 & 8 tacet

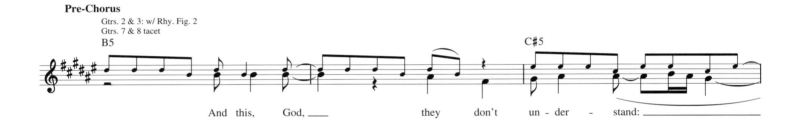

And this, God, _____ they don't un - der - stand:

_____ why what is _____ should

be. _____ Try to hide

_____ in the il - lu - sion that _____ they fight _____ and

Guitar Solo

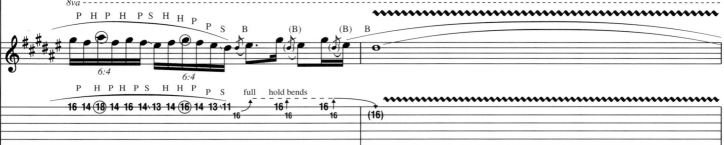

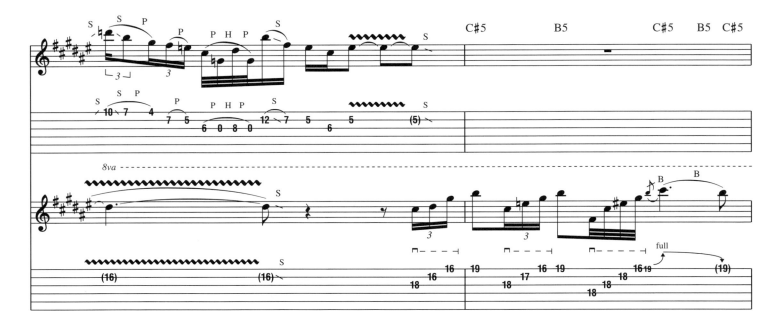

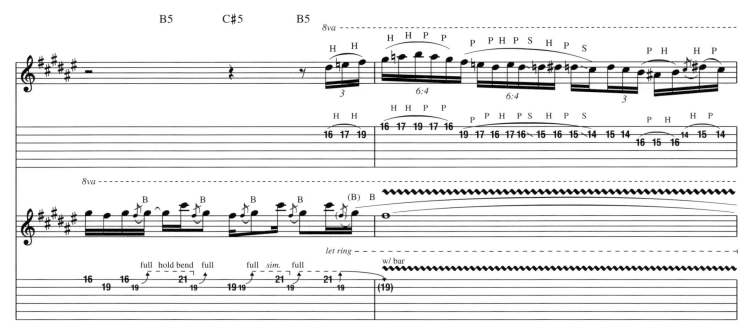

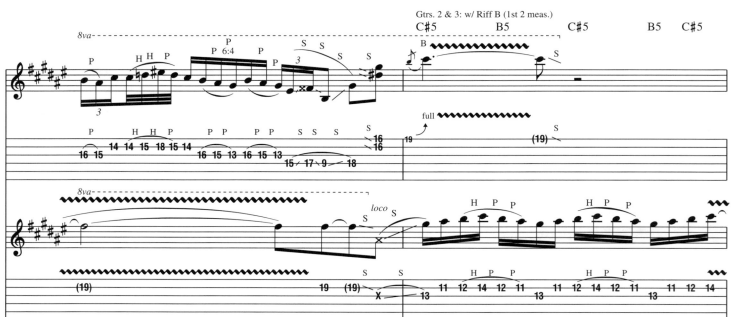

196

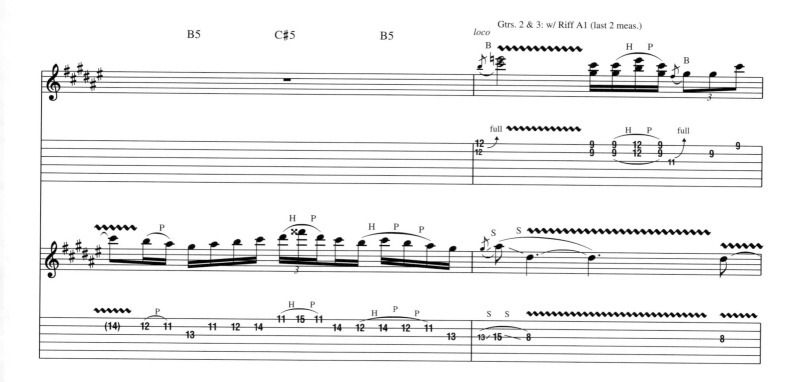

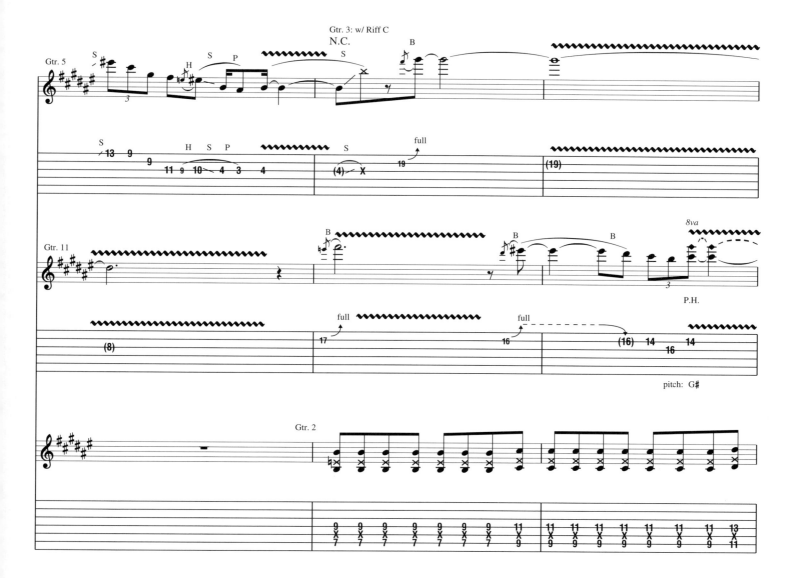

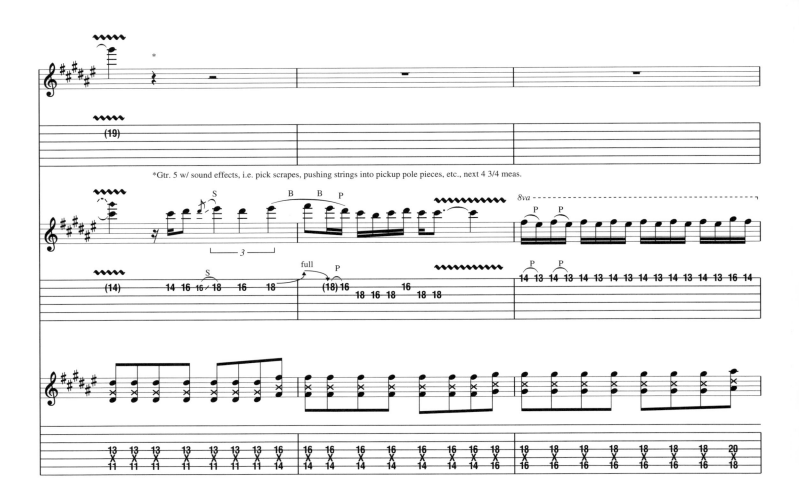

*Gtr. 5 w/ sound effects, i.e. pick scrapes, pushing strings into pickup pole pieces, etc., next 4 3/4 meas.

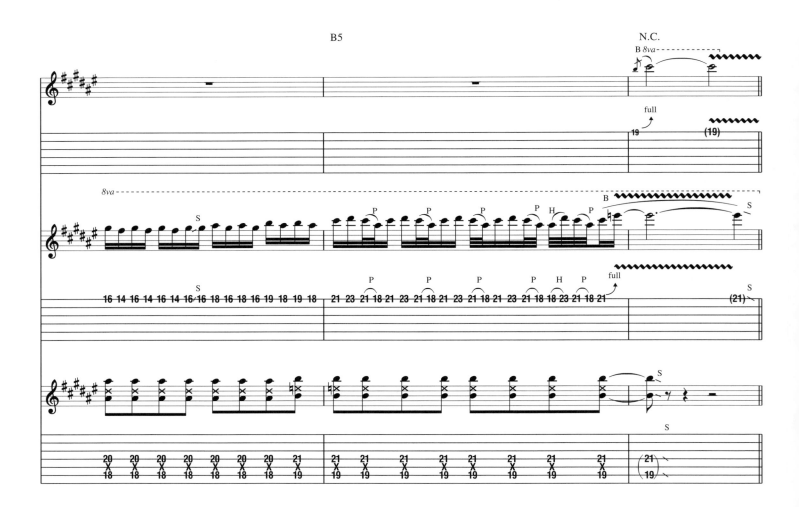

Gtr. 6: w/ Fill 2

C#5   B5   C#5 B5C#5   B5   C#5 B5

But my hands are reaching up unto the heavens, 'cause I wanna know what I could be.   A -

(Ah,

Chorus

N.C.

Gtr. 6: w/ Fill 2

live   in an A - sian sky.   A -

Gtr. 11 tacet

Gtr. 6: w/ Fill 2

live   in an A - sian sky.   A -

in an A - sian   sky.)

Gtr. 5

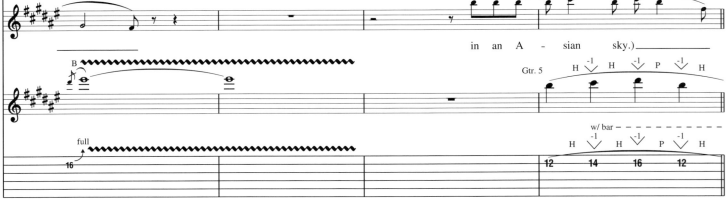

Outro-Chorus

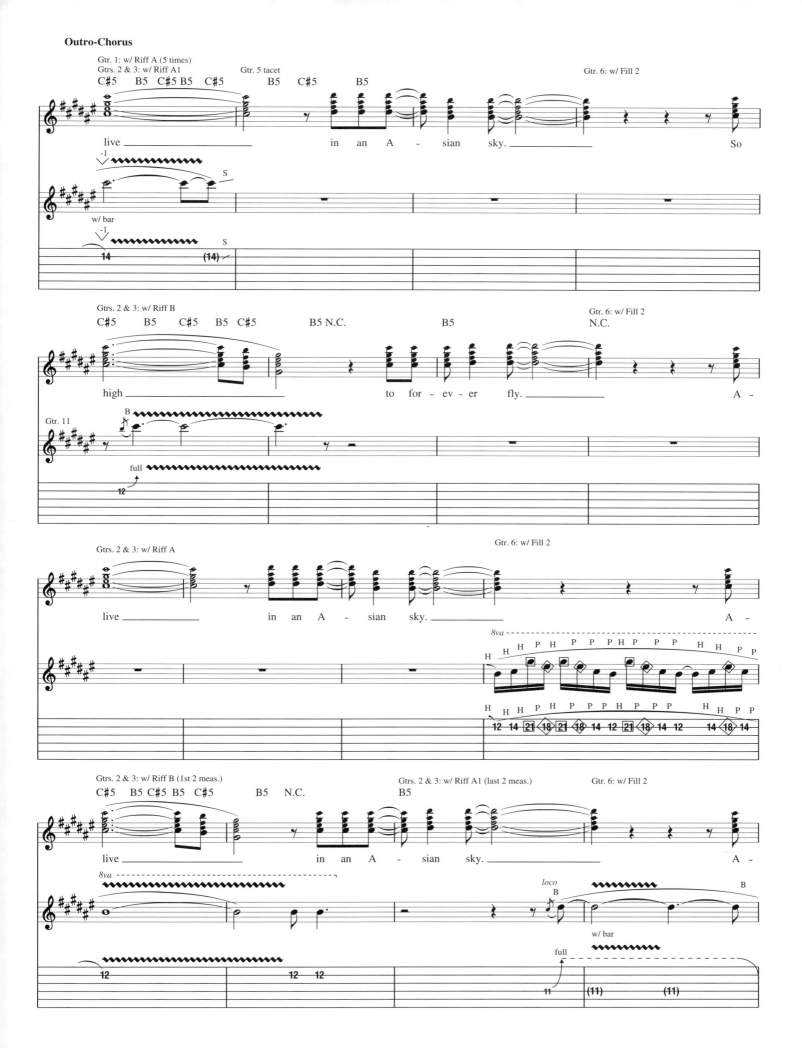

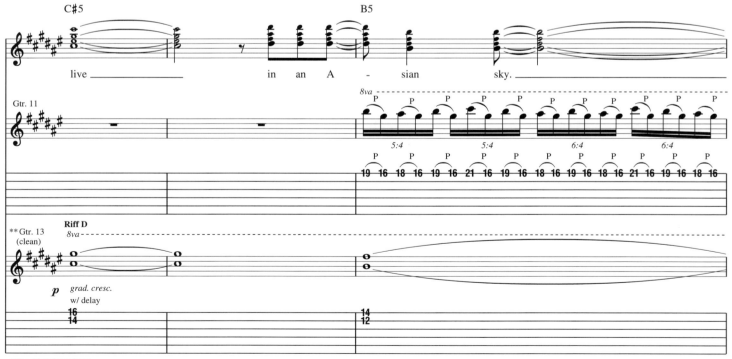

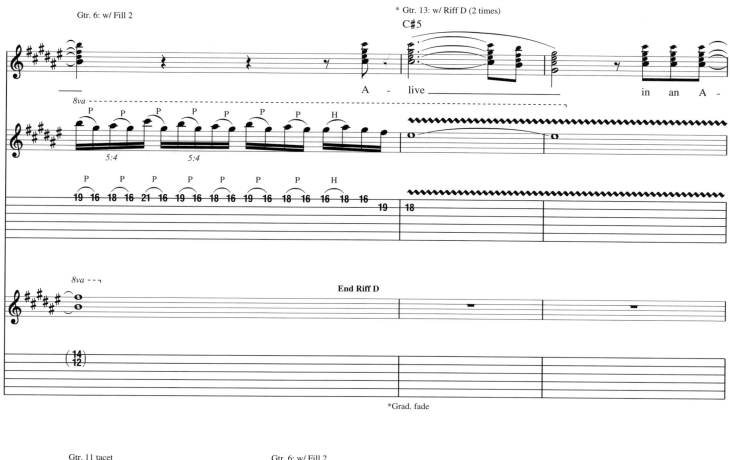

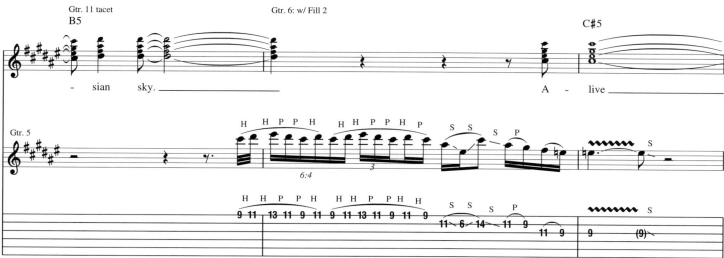

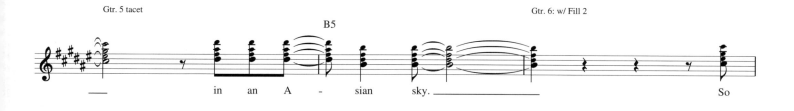

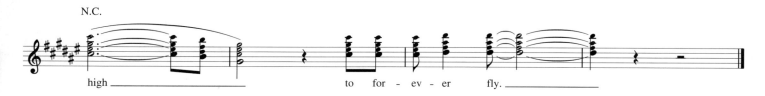

RECORDED VERSIONS

The Best Note-For-Note Transcriptions Available

ALL BOOKS INCLUDE TABLATURE

00690016 Will Ackerman Collection	$19.95
00690146 Aerosmith – Toys in the Attic	$19.95
00694865 Alice In Chains – Dirt	$19.95
00694932 Allman Brothers Band – Volume 1	$24.95
00694933 Allman Brothers Band – Volume 2	$24.95
00694934 Allman Brothers Band – Volume 3	$24.95
00694877 Chet Atkins – Guitars For All Seasons	$19.95
00690418 Best of Audio Adrenaline	$17.95
00694918 Randy Bachman Collection	$22.95
00690366 Bad Company Original Anthology - Bk 1	$19.95
00690367 Bad Company Original Anthology - Bk 2	$19.95
00694880 Beatles – Abbey Road	$19.95
00694863 Beatles – Sgt. Pepper's Lonely Hearts Club Band	$19.95
00690383 Beatles – Yellow Submarine	$19.95
00690174 Beck – Mellow Gold	$17.95
00690346 Beck – Mutations	$19.95
00690175 Beck – Odelay	$17.95
00694884 The Best of George Benson	$19.95
00692385 Chuck Berry	$19.95
00692200 Black Sabbath – We Sold Our Soul For Rock 'N' Roll	$19.95
00690115 Blind Melon – Soup	$19.95
00690305 Blink 182 – Dude Ranch	$19.95
00690028 Blue Oyster Cult – Cult Classics	$19.95
00690219 Blur	$19.95
00690168 Roy Buchanon Collection	$19.95
00690364 Cake – Songbook	$19.95
00690337 Jerry Cantrell – Boggy Depot	$19.95
00690293 Best of Steven Curtis Chapman	$19.95
00690043 Cheap Trick – Best Of	$19.95
00690171 Chicago – Definitive Guitar Collection	$22.95
00690415 Clapton Chronicles – Best of Eric Clapton	$17.95
00690393 Eric Clapton – Selections from Blues	$19.95
00660139 Eric Clapton – Journeyman	$19.95
00694869 Eric Clapton – Live Acoustic	$19.95
00694896 John Mayall/Eric Clapton – Bluesbreakers	$19.95
00690162 Best of the Clash	$19.95
00690166 Albert Collins – The Alligator Years	$16.95
00694940 Counting Crows – August & Everything After	$19.95
00690197 Counting Crows – Recovering the Satellites	$19.95
00694840 Cream – Disraeli Gears	$19.95
00690401 Creed – Human Clay	$19.95
00690352 Creed – My Own Prison	$19.95
00690184 dc Talk – Jesus Freak	$19.95
00690333 dc Talk – Supernatural	$19.95
00660186 Alex De Grassi Guitar Collection	$19.95
00690289 Best of Deep Purple	$17.95
00694831 Derek And The Dominos – Layla & Other Assorted Love Songs	$19.95
00690322 Ani Di Franco – Little Plastic Castle	$19.95
00690187 Dire Straits – Brothers In Arms	$19.95
00690191 Dire Straits – Money For Nothing	$24.95
00695382 The Very Best of Dire Straits – Sultans of Swing	$19.95
00660178 Willie Dixon – Master Blues Composer	$24.95
00690250 Best of Duane Eddy	$16.95
00690349 Eve 6	$19.95
00313164 Eve 6 – Horrorscope	$19.95
00690323 Fastball – All the Pain Money Can Buy	$19.95
00690089 Foo Fighters	$19.95
00690235 Foo Fighters – The Colour and the Shape	$19.95
00690394 Foo Fighters – There Is Nothing Left to Lose	$19.95
00690222 G3 Live – Satriani, Vai, Johnson	$22.95
00694807 Danny Gatton – 88 Elmira St	$19.95
00690438 Genesis Guitar Anthology	$19.95

00690127 Goo Goo Dolls – A Boy Named Goo	$19.95
00690338 Goo Goo Dolls – Dizzy Up the Girl	$19.95
00690117 John Gorka Collection	$19.95
00690114 Buddy Guy Collection Vol. A-J	$22.95
00690193 Buddy Guy Collection Vol. L-Y	$22.95
00694798 George Harrison Anthology	$19.95
00690068 Return Of The Hellecasters	$19.95
00692930 Jimi Hendrix – Are You Experienced?	$24.95
00692931 Jimi Hendrix – Axis: Bold As Love	$22.95
00692932 Jimi Hendrix – Electric Ladyland	$24.95
00690218 Jimi Hendrix – First Rays of the New Rising Sun	$27.95
00690038 Gary Hoey – Best Of	$19.95
00660029 Buddy Holly	$19.95
00690054 Hootie & The Blowfish – Cracked Rear View	$19.95
00694905 Howlin' Wolf	$19.95
00690136 Indigo Girls – 1200 Curfews	$22.95
00694938 Elmore James – Master Electric Slide Guitar	$19.95
00690167 Skip James Blues Guitar Collection	$16.95
00694833 Billy Joel For Guitar	$19.95
00694912 Eric Johnson – Ah Via Musicom	$19.95
00690169 Eric Johnson – Venus Isle	$22.95
00694799 Robert Johnson – At The Crossroads	$19.95
00693185 Judas Priest – Vintage Hits	$19.95
00690277 Best of Kansas	$19.95
00690073 B. B. King – 1950-1957	$24.95
00690098 B. B. King – 1958-1967	$24.95
00690444 B.B. King and Eric Clapton – Riding with the King	$19.95
00690134 Freddie King Collection	$17.95
00690157 Kiss – Alive	$19.95
00690163 Mark Knopfler/Chet Atkins – Neck and Neck	$19.95
00690296 Patty Larkin Songbook	$17.95
00690018 Living Colour – Best Of	$19.95
00694845 Yngwie Malmsteen – Fire And Ice	$19.95
00694956 Bob Marley – Legend	$19.95
00690283 Best of Sarah McLachlan	$19.95
00690382 Sarah McLachlan – Mirrorball	$19.95
00690354 Sarah McLachlan – Surfacing	$19.95
00690442 Matchbox 20 – Mad Season	$19.95
00690239 Matchbox 20 – Yourself or Someone Like You	$19.95
00690244 Megadeath – Cryptic Writings	$19.95
00690236 Mighty Mighty Bosstones – Let's Face It	$19.95
00690040 Steve Miller Band Greatest Hits	$19.95
00694802 Gary Moore – Still Got The Blues	$19.95
00694958 Mountain, Best Of	$19.95
00690448 MxPx – The Ever Passing Moment	$19.95
00694913 Nirvana – In Utero	$19.95
00694883 Nirvana – Nevermind	$19.95
00690026 Nirvana – Acoustic In New York	$19.95
00690121 Oasis – (What's The Story) Morning Glory	$19.95
00690204 Offspring, The – Ixnay on the Hombre	$17.95
00690203 Offspring, The – Smash	$17.95
00694830 Ozzy Osbourne – No More Tears	$19.95
00694855 Pearl Jam – Ten	$19.95
00690053 Liz Phair – Whip Smart	$19.95
00690176 Phish – Billy Breathes	$22.95
00690424 Phish – Farmhouse	$19.95
00690331 Phish – The Story of Ghost	$19.95
00690428 Pink Floyd – Dark Side of the Moon	$19.95
00693800 Pink Floyd – Early Classics	$19.95
00690456 P.O.D. – The Fundamental Elements of Southtown	$19.95
00694967 Police – Message In A Box Boxed Set	$70.00
00694974 Queen – A Night At The Opera	$19.95

00690395 Rage Against The Machine – The Battle of Los Angeles	$19
00690145 Rage Against The Machine – Evil Empire	$19
00690179 Rancid – And Out Come the Wolves	$22
00690055 Red Hot Chili Peppers – Bloodsugarsexmagik	$19
00690379 Red Hot Chili Peppers – Californication	$19
00690090 Red Hot Chili Peppers – One Hot Minute	$22
00694937 Jimmy Reed – Master Bluesman	$19
00694899 R.E.M. – Automatic For The People	$19
00690260 Jimmie Rodgers Guitar Collection	$19
00690014 Rolling Stones – Exile On Main Street	$24
00690186 Rolling Stones – Rock & Roll Circus	$19
00690135 Otis Rush Collection	$19
00690031 Santana's Greatest Hits	$19
00690150 Son Seals – Bad Axe Blues	$17
00690128 Seven Mary Three – American Standards	$19
00120105 Kenny Wayne Shepherd – Ledbetter Heights	$19
00120123 Kenny Wayne Shepherd – Trouble Is	$19
00690196 Silverchair – Freak Show	$19
00690130 Silverchair – Frogstomp	$19
00690041 Smithereens – Best Of	$19
00690385 Sonicflood	$19
00694885 Spin Doctors – Pocket Full Of Kryptonite	$19
00694921 Steppenwolf, The Best Of	$22
00694957 Rod Stewart – Acoustic Live	$22
00690021 Sting – Fields Of Gold	$19
00690242 Suede – Coming Up	$19
00694824 Best Of James Taylor	$16
00690238 Third Eye Blind	$19
00690403 Third Eye Blind – Blue	$19
00690267 311	$19
00690030 Toad The Wet Sprocket	$19
00690228 Tonic – Lemon Parade	$19
00690295 Tool – Aenima	$19
00690039 Steve Vai – Alien Love Secrets	$24
00690172 Steve Vai – Fire Garden	$24
00690023 Jimmie Vaughan – Strange Pleasures	$19
00690370 Stevie Ray Vaughan and Double Trouble – The Real Deal: Greatest Hits Volume 2	$22
00690455 Stevie Ray Vaughan – Blues at Sunrise	$19
00660136 Stevie Ray Vaughan – In Step	$19
00690417 Stevie Ray Vaughan – Live at Carnegie Hall	$19
00694835 Stevie Ray Vaughan – The Sky Is Crying	$19
00694776 Vaughan Brothers – Family Style	$19
00120026 Joe Walsh – Look What I Did...	$24
00694789 Muddy Waters – Deep Blues	$19
00690071 Weezer	$19
00690286 Weezer – Pinkerton	$19
00690447 Who, The – Best of	$24
00694970 Who, The – Definitive Collection A-E	$24
00694971 Who, The – Definitive Collection F-Li	$24
00694972 Who, The – Definitive Collection Lo-R	$24
00694973 Who, The – Definitive Collection S-Y	$24
00690319 Stevie Wonder Hits	$17

GUITAR *signature licks*

Signature Licks book/CD packs provide a step-by-step breakdown of "right from the record" riffs, licks, and solos so you can jam along with your favorite bands. They contain full performance notes and an overview of each artist or group's style, with note-for-note transcriptions in notes and tab. The CDs feature full-band demos at both normal and slow speeds.

ACOUSTIC GUITAR OF '60S AND '70S
00695024 Book/CD Pack $19.95

ACOUSTIC GUITAR OF '80S AND '90S
00695033 Book/CD Pack $19.95

AEROSMITH 1973-1979
00695106 Book/CD Pack..........$19.95

AEROSMITH 1979-1998
00695219 Book/CD Pack $19.95

BEATLES BASS
00695283 Book/CD Pack $19.95

THE BEATLES FAVORITES
00695096 Book/CD Pack $19.95

THE BEATLES HITS
00695049 Book/CD Pack $19.95

BEST OF THE BEATLES FOR ACOUSTIC GUITAR
00695453 Book/CD Pack..........$19.95

BEST OF GEORGE BENSON
00695418 Book/CD Pack..........$19.95

THE BEST OF BLACK SABBATH
00695249 Book/CD Pack $19.95

BEST OF AGGRO-METAL
00695592 Book/CD Pack $19.95

BEST OF JAZZ GUITAR
00695586 Book/CD Pack..........$24.95

BEST OF R&B
00695288 Book/CD Pack..........$19.95

BEST OF ROCK 'N' ROLL GUITAR
00695559 Book/CD Pack $19.95

BLUES GUITAR CLASSICS
00695177 Book/CD Pack $19.95

THE BEST OF ERIC CLAPTON
00695038 Book/CD Pack $24.95

ERIC CLAPTON – THE BLUESMAN
00695040 Book/CD Pack $19.95

ERIC CLAPTON – FROM THE ALBUM UNPLUGGED
00695250 Book/CD Pack $19.95

THE BEST OF CREAM
00695251 Book/CD Pack $19.95

BEST OF DEEP PURPLE
00695625 Book/CD Pack $19.95

THE BEST OF DEF LEPPARD
00696516 Book/CD Pack $19.95

THE DOORS
00695373 Book/CD Pack $19.95

BEST OF FOO FIGHTERS
00695481 Book/CD Pack......$19.95

GREATEST GUITAR SOLOS OF ALL TIME
00695301 Book/CD Pack..........$19.95

GUITAR INSTRUMENTAL HITS
00695309 Book/CD Pack..........$17.95

GUITAR RIFFS OF THE '60S
00695218 Book/CD pack..........$17.95

GUITAR RIFFS OF THE '70S
00695158 Book/CD Pack $17.95

THE BEST OF GUNS N' ROSES
00695183 Book/CD Pack..........$19.95

THE BEST OF BUDDY GUY
00695186 Book/CD Pack..........$19.95

JIMI HENDRIX
00696560 Book/CD Pack $22.95

ERIC JOHNSON
00699317 Book/CD Pack $19.95

ROBERT JOHNSON
00695264 Book/CD Pack..........$19.95

B.B. KING – THE DEFINITIVE COLLECTION
00695635 Book/CD Pack $19.95

MARK KNOPFLER
00695178 Book/CD Pack..........$19.95

MEGADETH
00695041 Book/CD Pack $19.95

WES MONTGOMERY
00695387 Book/CD Pack..........$19.95

MOTOWN BASS
00695506 Book/CD Pack $16.95

PINK FLOYD – EARLY CLASSICS
00695566 Book/CD Pack..........$19.95

THE GUITARS OF ELVIS
00696507 Book/CD Pack..........$19.95

BEST OF QUEEN
00695097 Book/CD Pack $19.95

BEST OF RAGE AGAINST THE MACHINE
00695480 Book/CD Pack $19.95

THE RED HOT CHILI PEPPERS
00695173 Book/CD Pack $19.95

THE BEST OF THE RED HOT CHILI PEPPERS FOR BASS
00695285 Book/CD Pack $19.95

THE ROLLING STONES
00695079 Book/CD Pack..........$19.95

THE BEST OF JOE SATRIANI
00695216 Book/CD Pack $19.95

BEST OF SILVERCHAIR
00695488 Book/CDPack $19.95

STEVE VAI
00673247 Book/CD Pack $22.95

STEVE VAI – ALIEN LOVE SECRETS: THE NAKED VAMPS
00695223 Book/CD Pack..........$19.95

STEVE VAI – FIRE GARDEN: THE NAKED VAMPS
00695166 Book/CD Pack..........$19.95

STEVIE RAY VAUGHAN
00699316 Book/CD Pack $19.95

THE GUITAR STYLE OF STEVIE RAY VAUGHAN
00695155 Book/CD Pack $19.95

THE WHO
00695561 Book/CD Pack..........$19.95

1001

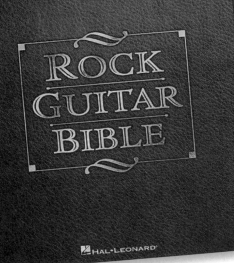